S0-AZX-375

Leader's Guide

UMI

God's Vision or Television?

How Television Influences What We Believe

CARL JEFFREY WRIGHT

Urban Ministries, Inc.
The African American Christian Publishing
& Communications Co.

Writer: C. Jeffrey Wright

Publisher
UMI (Urban Ministries, Inc.)
P.O. Box 436987
Chicago, IL 60643-6897
1-800-860-8642
www.urbanministries.com
First Edition
First Printing
ISBN: 0-940955-91-1

Copyright © 2004 by UMI (Urban Ministries, Inc.). All rights reserved. No part of this publication may be reproduced, stored in a retrieval system, or transmitted in any form or by any means, electronic—mechanical, photocopy, recording, or otherwise—except for brief quotations in printed reviews without prior written permission of the publisher or the holder of the copyright. Printed in the United States of America.

Table of Contents

Preface

In one shocking second, the power of American television was revealed to the world in a Super Bowl halftime show. MTV, the cable network that produced the show, and CBS, the broadcast network that aired the football game, are both owned by Viacom, one of the largest media companies in the world. This is the same network that recently bought BET, owns the largest children's television network, Nickelodeon, as well as UPN, and many other television and media properties. Understanding this concentration of media in the hands of a few giant corporations and the impact they have on American life and, in particular, the image of African Americans and Christians, is critical.

The debate over the influence of television should now be over; it is time to recognize this influence and respond to it. Some may want to join the ranks of those who, as media activists, seek to change the programming choices of these corporate giants. Others have organized letter-writing campaigns and boycotts targeting advertisers whose commercials and products pay for the things we see on television. Still others may simply want to change their own viewing behaviors, but the Bible calls us all to response.

Purpose of the Book. *God's Vision or Television?* seeks to bring some understanding of the influence of television upon our lives and the need for a biblical response to its power. African Americans watch more hours of television weekly than any other group and therefore need to be especially aware of the powers and dangers of this medium. Since its invention, television has given a partial and inaccurate picture of the African American population and virtually all other ethnic minority groups. Christians and the biblical worldview, once at the heart of nearly every show, are now virtually limited to religious broadcasts; and sadly, some of these programs are among the lowest quality television being aired. God is not well represented on television today.

This book provides insights that will encourage you to change your viewing habits and become more aware of how television may influence how you see the world. It examines television's programming, management, and biases along with a selection of Bible passages that illustrate the need to keep God at the center of your vision. Several charts, notes, and references are included to provide statistical information on this industry and sources for additional research or response. Each chapter ends with some suggested actions to consider and encouragement to make a difference in your personal life and the world around you.

The Leader's Guide. This leader's guide accompanies the book and contains a discussion guide for each chapter of *God's Vision or Television?* It is designed for leaders who use the book as a text for group Bible studies, Sunday School electives, Vacation Bible School, and special church retreats or studies. It can also be used for leading family devotions or other reading group activities. Each chapter contains a suggested lesson plan and detailed suggestions for small group activities. Answers to Bible study questions in the related student workbook are at the end of each chapter.

The Student Workbook. A separate student workbook accompanies the student book, *God's Vision or Television?* Each chapter of the workbook contains an in-depth Bible study application. The application consists of five Bible discovery exercises, a church Ministry Application, and a Personal Application.

In summary, while there are many ways to use this book and its study guides, the main purpose is that Christians become sensitized to the power and influence of television and move from passively watching this medium to actively challenging and monitoring the visions that it tells us to pursue.

Introduction

Television is influential. In the United States, it is the main thing we do—and we "do" a lot of it. The average American sits in front of the screen *watching* TV for what amounts to one entire day (about 20 hours) (Peers 2004, B1). As Americans, we are different for many reasons, but the habitual viewing of television is probably what separates us from most people in the world today. We rely on television for our vision. One writer has defined vision as "a clear mental image of what could be, fueled by the conviction that it should be" (Stanley 2001, 18). Vision, in America, comes from television. Television has given us a vision, and we believe in it.

Americans spend more time getting their visions from television than any other people in the world, and African Americans watch more of it than anyone else. We spend many more hours a week watching this medium than the average American, and its impact on our vision has been devastating. The televising of certain aspects of African American culture, a relatively recent phenomena, has changed the world's youth culture. The words *urban, hip-hop,* and *bling, bling* define the music, dress, and lifestyle of teens and young adults across racial and geographic boundaries. Unfortunately, this vision, or televised lifestyle, includes far more violence, drugs, sex, and vulgar language than most people would care to see expressed in our youth.

Ironically, religious television, including African American preaching programs, has had nearly as much additional exposure and for about the same length of time as the music and rap videos that so many complain about. The growth of cable and satellite television has produced more religious programming than ever. The major impact of these religious shows seems to be the multiplication of religious television shows, but no visible difference in the culture. The religion of materialism and consumption has developed to the highest degree in human history through television.

In some instances the message of acquisitive consumerism, which is communicated through the prosperous lifestyles, luxurious cars, expensive clothes, and flashy jewelry of television's preachers, is exactly the same as the music video stars. But the music videos have better beats and seem to get more converts. Actually, it is sometimes difficult to tell the difference between the two because regardless of whether they are preaching or rapping, what we see is the same: the accumulation and display of wealth, conspicuous consumption, and a lifestyle that suggests that the goal is to create the highest amount of comfort before death comes.

Though it is not a specific focus of this book, television's influence on politics has been most profound. We now choose virtually all key elected officials based primarily on what they look like on television and how much money they spend on television advertising. In the presidential election of 2000, the candidates so closely resembled each other that for White Americans it was a virtual tie. African Americans could only distinguish the two candidates by the labels they wore; because television has taught us that Republicans are racists and Democrats are not, we had a basis for choice other than appearance.

The irony of this is that ideologically, African Americans have far more in common with Republicans than Democrats. According to author Neil Postman, this is a world where "discourse is conducted largely through visual imagery, which is to say that television gives us a conversation in images not words" (1985). The fact is that African American beliefs about morality, school choice, crime, big government, and other political platform issues are largely Republican. This is completely overwhelmed by the vision of a pickup truck dragging a Black man, or a Black male athlete going to jail for having sex with a White woman, while a White corporate executive pays a $5 million bail to go home after being charged with looting billions of dollars from millions of people. Racism produces unforgettable imagery and the visual lifestyle differences that result from it overwhelm all other political ideas.

The influence of television news is unquestioned. Although the news habit is purely a function of technology and there is no single set of important events that occurs each day that we all need to know about, televi-

sion has led us to believe that a person who has not watched the news is an uninformed and unintelligent person. The news habit is a creation of the technology; it's a media event. There is no news of the day in cultures that are not trapped by television. The point here is not that important things do not happen, but rather that the decision about what is important and the process by which you get this information is not the product of some quest for absolute truth; but simply another way to get you to watch television. A lot of "important" things that happened were not on the news, like the half billion new Christians in Africa and the shift of Christianity from the White West to the "Brown" Southern Hemisphere.

The total purpose of television is entertainment. The goal—to sell you products.

Television has become dominated by a few very large conglomerates that have now acquired control of virtually all media. By media we mean the means of communicating information or entertainment to large audiences at the same time. The various forms include newspapers, magazines, books, television programs, movies, music, and digital versions of these forms, which can be contained on various types of objects such as CDs or DVDs and can also be made directly available over the Internet (so-called "e-content").

The corporations that bring you this content have as their overriding purpose the goal of "increasing shareholder value." They want to grow larger and more profitable because that increases the value of the company and creates wealth for management and for the people who own stock in them. It does not matter whether the show is good or bad in any moral sense of the word. The only question is: Does it attract and retain viewers so that commercials can be sold for more money?

A consequence of this is that much of television today is of very low moral value, though the economic value is high. The most highly watched television programs—the Super Bowl, the Oscars, the Grammy Awards, and the final episodes of *Sex and the City* and *Friends*—all offer very little, if any, redeeming moral content. But the many millions spent for 30 and 60 second commercials during these programs show that they have tremendous value to the companies that own them.

Through television, the country today has exalted "free market capitalism" as its highest value. With very few exceptions, primarily illegal drugs, it is OK to sell anything in the U.S. The law of the market has superceded biblical law, which is the actual root of law in Western society. The nation has evolved, or perhaps devolved, to a non-moral based system that protects not the good of society or the development of health and respect for the individual, but rather the protection of the right to make money.

This protection meant that government regulation of the use of the airwaves and the content of television has been ineffective, except in the most minimal of ways. Anything can be shown and is being shown. The president of Viacom appeared before Congress after his company's televised halftime sex show at the 2004 Super Bowl and stated that while he felt the show was inappropriate and possibly offensive, it probably was not *illegal* under the vague decency standards of the FCC. The consequences for society and its children are that parents have to protect them or they have to fend for themselves.

The result is increased violence, drug use, alcoholism, suicide, and perverted and extramarital sexual activity. The definitions of "free speech" and the "rights" of people and companies have been stretched to include behavior that in another time would have been prosecuted.

Black people and other minorities have been victimized personally by the visual stereotypes that make them poster children for the most negative aspects of behavior and lifestyle in programming, music videos, and television news. This follows a centuries old belief system in Western/ European/American philosophy and thought that evolutionary hierarchy of man begins with Europeans and descends to various people of color with Africans at the lowest level of humanity—and animals not far behind. Reinforcing this social mythology through television programs and films that depict a reality that supports this view, has been the most insidious effect of television on Black people.

What all Christians—Black and White—should be doing is supporting the explosion of Christianity in the Southern Hemisphere and addressing the AIDS crisis here and in Africa. This is a divine vision for the entire church and a mandate for the Black church. Paul boldly wrote, "if any pro-

vide not for his own,... he...is worse than an infidel" (1 Timothy 5:8, KJV). Isn't the Black church called to address the needs of the church in Africa, and what about the millions of AIDS orphans there? African Americans have annual household incomes of nearly $700 billion, more than all the Black population of Africa combined. While it is true that we have many problems here, our vision should also include helping those who were left behind. Why do we need a television special to tell us this is a serious problem that needs to be addressed? We must redirect our time and attention to the vision that God has put before us.

Using the case studies and Scripture references in this Leader's Guide, you can facilitate an examination of these issues that should lead participants to a deeper level of commitment to the Word of God and more diligence in guarding minds from the negative influences of television.

CHAPTER ONE

TELEVISION–Is What You See Really What You Get?

Format for Sessions of 90 Minutes or More

PART ONE		PART TWO*	
MIN.	ACTIVITY	MIN.	ACTIVITY
5	Prayer	5	Case Study
10	Introduction	30	Small Group Study
15	Scripture Discussion	10	Small Group Presentations
10	Chapter Highlights	18	Large Group Discussion
		3	Prayer

*For sessions of less than 90 minutes, use PART ONE only, and assign the case study as homework. *To complete the activities in PART TWO, each participant will need the related workbook that contains the exercises for the small groups, study worksheets for the Ministry Application, and space for journalizing related to the Personal Application.*

LESSON AIM: At the end of this two–part training session, the participant should be able to: a) understand the reliability of the Bible compared to television and other media; b) explain the economic model of the television industry; c) discuss how concentration in the media has reduced media ownership

to a few companies; d) identify other sources of news and information besides television, and know the importance of using them; e) identify biblical passages that prophesy the coming Messiah; f) discuss ways in which the local church can more effectively guard our faith from falsehood.

I. PART ONE

A. PRAYER
Open the session with prayer, including the lesson aim.

B. INTRODUCTION
In this opening session, first present the topic of study—prophecy and biblical truth. It might be useful to include background information from the Introduction to the Student Book or the Introduction to the Leader's Guide. If available, some of the statistics can be used to create overhead transparencies or PowerPoint slides for this purpose. It might also be helpful to review the format of the workbook that they will be using in the small group discussions. Then introduce the lesson for today—Is What You See Really What You Get?

C. SCRIPTURE DISCUSSION
Read Micah 5:2–5; Isaiah 7:14; and Matthew 1:21–23. Alternate between leader and group. Then discuss the following questions:
1. Which verse identifies the birthplace of Christ?
2. How does Micah describe the relationship between Christ the Messiah and His followers?
3. What are the three elements of the sign prophesied in Isaiah 7:14?
4. What is the meaning of the name Immanuel?
5. What were the circumstances that Joseph faced when he encountered the angel?
6. What was confirmed to him by the angel's message?

D. CHAPTER HIGHLIGHTS
Explain that the chapter focuses on believing the prophecies of God rather

than believing the things we see on television. Ask for volunteers to share how they get their news and information; then ask about how many hours a week they watch television. Then, using chapter one as background, provide a general overview of the points made in the chapter. Be sure to discuss the following questions:

1. Why can we trust the prophecies of the Bible?
2. What are some of the reasons that television cannot be considered a reliable source for news and information?
3. What is the economic model of television? How does television make money for its owners?
4. How many major companies own and control television and most other forms of mass media? Name some of the leading companies and some types of media they own.
5. What are some specific ways (presented in the chapter) that we can guard against the distortion of truth by the media?
6. Why should African Americans be especially concerned about distortions in the media?

Ask the group to reflect on the Howard Dean presidential candidacy (from the introductory case study). How might you have determined in advance that his presidential candidacy would not succeed? What role did the Internet play in predicting that he would become the Democratic presidential candidate for 2004?

Provide enough time for them to discuss this situation and how the guidelines presented in the chapter might apply to it.

II. PART TWO

To complete the activities in PART TWO, each participant will need a student workbook that contains the Bible Application exercises, worksheets for the Ministry Application, and spaces for journalizing in response to the Personal Application. Answers to the Bible Application exercises are included in this Leader's Guide.

A. CASE STUDY

1. Introduction

Explain that the case study in the workbook provides an opportunity to apply the principles presented in the chapter to a real–life story. Political campaigns present the special problem of distortion by the media, and exaggeration and distortion by the candidates themselves.

2. Procedure

Select Small Group Leaders. Ask for volunteers or select five group leaders. Then assign each group leader a number (1–5). (This can also be done beforehand.) Ask each group leader to write their number on a large sheet of paper so that they can easily be seen.

Divide into Small Groups. Inform the participants that they will be forming five groups. Each group will study a different set of questions related to the case study and biblical prophecy, and will present their findings to the larger group at the end of the group study period. The set of questions to be studied should correspond with the group numbers as follows:

Group #1: Old Testament Prophecy
Group #2: New Testament Prophetic Fulfillment
Group #3: Biblical Truth—What Does the Bible Define as Truth?
Group #4: The Enemy of Truth
Group #5: The Response of the Christian

Ask the class (excluding the group leaders) to count off by fives. Then have them join the small group leader that is displaying the number they were just assigned. Inform them of the meeting places for each of the groups. (These locations can be printed beforehand, to facilitate a smoother transition.) Then allow the participants to assemble into the smaller groups at their designated meeting places.

B. SMALL GROUP STUDY

1. Small Group Leaders Allocate Questions

For each exercise, there are five "discovery" questions and a summary

question. Therefore, each small group will have one exercise to complete, and that exercise will involve answering five questions and a summary question.

Assign one discovery question to each person in the group. If there are more people than questions, allow people to work on questions in twos or threes, etc. If there are more questions than people, assign more than one question per person.

Don't consider the summary question at this time, since it will be discussed by the small group at the end of the small group study time, and it will be used as a basis for the small group presentation to the larger group. Ask each person (or pair, etc.) to answer their assigned question. If they divide into pairs, etc., they will need to elect a recorder that will summarize the smaller group's discussion when the entire class reconvenes. They can write their answers on paper or index cards cards that they will use as prompts when presenting their answers to the larger group.

2. Share Insights
After 10 minutes, ask the small group participants to come together in their groups. Allow each one to tell the question that he/she had and his/her answer to it. Then allow 5–18 minutes to discuss the summary question as a group. Designate someone who will summarize the small group discussion and report it to the larger group. Remind the designated person that he/she will only have one minute to present.

C. LARGE GROUP PRESENTATIONS
1. Large Group Leader
Reconvene the Group. Call the groups back together. If they are in different locations of the building, consider sending someone to each location or using another method of notifying them that time is up.

Explain the Procedure. Explain that a representative of each small group will share that group's reflections on prophecy and truth with the larger group. Then the large group, together, can discuss the Ministry Application and reflect on making a practical application of what has been learned.

Remind Small Group Representatives of the Time. Remind the small group representatives that they should try to summarize their group's discussion in one minute. Be sure that the small group presenters connect their presentations to both the case study of Howard Dean and/or to other political candidates. During this first session, they probably have not become accustomed to the process yet. Therefore, without extending their time limit too much, it may be necessary to pose questions that require them to relate their small group presentations to the case study and generalize it to other real–life situations. The respective small group emphasis should be on helping people to:

Group #1: See the importance of Old Testament prophecy

Group #2: Know that Christ validated Himself through prophecy

Group #3: Know that God's Word is truth

Group #4: Use the Scripture as a guide for truth

Group #5: Guard your faith with the Word of God

Be sure that they relate some of the Scriptures from the exercises to each of the topics above.

2. Ministry Application

Ask each participant to locate the Ministry Application worksheet in his/her workbook. Provide time (5–7 minutes) for either the large group to work together or for each participant to complete their own worksheet. Ask for volunteers to share their insights.

3. Personal Application

Call their attention to the spaces for journalizing in the workbook. Ask them, between this session and the next, to think about the Personal Application (exercise #7) and to read chapter two.

D. PRAYER

Hold hands and, in a circle, ask for specific prayer requests. Then ask for several volunteers to pray while keeping the prayer requests in mind.

ANSWERS TO BIBLE APPLICATION EXERCISES

1. Old Testament Prophecy

a. God will defeat Satan with a mortal wound (crush [his] head, Genesis 3:15, NLT).

b. Jesus the Messiah will not decay in the grave but be resurrected.

c. Jesus would be born of a virgin.

d. Jesus would be betrayed for 30 pieces of silver.

e. Details of the crucifixion are described including the casting of lots for Jesus' clothes, His bones not being broken, His thirst, and the piercing of His hands and feet.

f. SUMMARY ANSWER: Old Testament prophecies indicate the manner and place of Jesus' birth, betrayal, and death. The prophetic details of the crucifixion of Christ are complete and the events occurred in the exact manner that the prophets foretold.

2. New Testament Prophetic Fulfillment

a. Jesus was born of a virgin.

b. Like the serpent Moses lifted on a wooden pole that healed all who looked at it after suffering a deadly snakebite, with His own crucifixion, Jesus enables all who look to Him in believing faith to be saved.

c. Jesus compares the ministry of John the Baptist with Elijah.

d. Jonah was in the belly of the fish three days just as Jesus was in the grave three days.

e. The crucifixion of Christ followed the prophecy of Psalm 22:15–18.

f. SUMMARY ANSWER: Jesus referred to Old Testament Scriptures that He knew were familiar to His audience to give them evidence and proof that He was the Messiah.

3. Biblical Truth—What Does the Bible Define as Truth?

a. The Word is truth.

b. Truth stands the test of time; lies are soon exposed.

c. The Word was God and was with God, and the Word became flesh and dwelt among us.

d. Jesus defines Himself as the living embodiment of truth.

e. God must be worshiped in Spirit and in truth.

f. SUMMARY ANSWER: The Bible and the presence of the Holy Spirit in the life of believers are guides to truth. Unbelievers do not have the presence of the Holy Spirit and are open to deception if they are not following God's Word.

4. The Enemy of Truth
a. Satan, the God of this world, has blinded the minds of unbelievers.
b. People have rejected the truth and embraced lies instead.
c. As the father of lies, Satan lies through the media.
d. The enemy uses confusion in our thought life and false ideas in the media.
e. We resist the Holy Spirit and become deaf to the truth.
f. SUMMARY ANSWER: Believers should always compare what is presented as truth in the media with the Word of God. You should also keep in mind that the goal of much of television is entertainment. Therefore, it is important to review other sources to get a more complete understanding of news and events.

5. The Response of the Christian
a. Never oppose the truth, but stand for the truth at all times.
b. Study the Word of God so that you will be able to discern truth.
c. Follow the example of the Bereans, compare every message to the Word of God.
d. Be bold about proclaiming the truth everywhere.
e. Hold on to the truth and become more like Christ.
f. SUMMARY ANSWER: Students should use the Scriptures to show how God's Word applies to a news story. For example, God's Word says homosexuality is sin (see Leviticus 18:22; Romans 1:26–28), so reports on the fairness or rights of homosexuals should be considered in light of God's Word.

6. Ministry Application
A church study group that examines current events in light of biblical truth can lead to deeper examination of the Scriptures and the practical application of the faith in everyday life.

CHAPTER TWO

TELEVISION—God's Promises and TV's Promises

Format for Sessions of 90 Minutes or More

PART ONE		PART TWO*	
MIN.	ACTIVITY	MIN.	ACTIVITY
5	Prayer	5	Case Study
10	Personal Reflections	30	Small Group Study
15	Scripture Discussion	10	Small Group Presentations
10	Chapter Highlights	18	Large Group Discussion
		3	Prayer

*For sessions of less than 90 minutes, use PART ONE only, and assign the case study as homework. *To complete the activities in PART TWO, each participant will need the workbook that accompanies the student book.*

LESSON AIM: At the end of this two-part training session, the participant should be able to: a) describe the way God confirmed His promise of a Messiah through the witness of Simeon and Anna; b) recognize that television advertising presents false promises; c) understand the differences between contentment and excessive consumption; d) make a renewed commitment to keep their word.

I. PART ONE

A. PRAYER
Open the session with prayer, including the lesson aim.

B. PERSONAL REFLECTIONS
Last time, participants were asked to make personal applications of the material covered in the last session, using exercise #7 of chapter one. Allow time for volunteers to share the results of this Personal Application. Then introduce the lesson for today—God's Promises and TV's Promises.

C. SCRIPTURE DISCUSSION
Read Luke 2:25–38. Alternate between leader and group. Then discuss the following questions:
1. How does the Scripture describe Simeon and Anna, and what made them reliable witnesses?
2. What was God's promise to Simeon? What was Simeon's prophecy to Mary and Joseph?
3. Why was the Baby Jesus brought to the temple?
4. What was Anna's prophecy about Jesus?
5. Why were Simeon and Anna at the temple?

D. CHAPTER HIGHLIGHTS
Explain that the chapter focuses on God's promises as compared to the promises that come from television, particularly advertising. Ask them to provide examples of promises from television ads that are questionable or unbelievable. Also ask them to give examples of how overconsumption can lead to dissatisfaction and unhappiness. A discussion of contentment is presented, and the chapter contrasts contentment with affluenza, an addiction to consumption. Then, use the chapter as background to provide a general overview of the points made. Be sure to discuss questions such as:
1. Does God use "bait and switch" like the world?
2. Do television ads seek to fulfill needs or simply create needs?

3. What is the phenomena of "neuromarketing" and what are its risks?
4. Has the increase in credit card debt helped the economic position of African Americans?
5. Should disposable income be used to invest in what we want or what we need?

Have the group consider the situation of Mr. and Mrs. Williams (from the workbook case study). Expand the discussion by asking the class to give other examples of people who have been misled by television advertising. Provide enough time for them to explore these situations and discuss how the guidelines presented in the chapter might apply to them.

II. PART TWO

To complete the activities in PART TWO, participants will need the workbook that accompanies the student book.

A. CASE STUDY

1. Introduction

Explain that the case study in the workbook provides an opportunity to apply the principles presented in the chapter to a real–life story. The Williams family has become trapped in debt after purchasing a luxury SUV. They are constantly anxious about making the payments.

2. Procedure

Select Small Group Leaders. Ask for volunteers or select five group leaders. Then assign each group leader a number (1–5). (This can also be done beforehand.) Ask the group leaders to write their number on a large sheet of paper so that it can easily be seen.

Divide into Small Groups. Inform them that they will assemble into five small groups. Each group will study a different set of questions related to the case study and will present their findings to the larger group at the end of the

group study period. The set of questions to be studied should correspond with the group numbers as follows:

Group #1: The Nature of God's Promises
Group #2: God's Promises for Those Who Keep His Commands
Group #3: Keeping Your Promises
Group #4: The Enemy of God's Promises
Group #5: The False Promises of the Enemy

Have the participants count off by fives. Then ask them to join the small group leader that is displaying their respective assigned numbers. Inform them of the meeting places for each of the groups. (These locations can also be printed beforehand to facilitate a smoother transition.) Then allow the participants to assemble into the smaller groups at their designated meeting places.

B. SMALL GROUP STUDY

1. Small Group Leaders Allocate Questions

For each exercise, there are five "discovery" questions and a summary question. Therefore, each small group will have one exercise to complete, and that exercise will involve answering five questions and a summary question. Assign one discovery question to each person in the group. If there are more people than questions, allow people to work on questions in twos or threes, etc. If there are more questions than people, assign more than one question per person.

Don't consider the summary question at this time; the small group will discuss it at the end of the group study time, and it will be used as a basis for the small group's presentation to the larger group. Ask each person (or pair, etc.) to answer the assigned question.

2. Share Insights

After 10 minutes, ask the small group participants to come together in their groups. Allow each one to tell the question that he/she had and the answer to it. Then allow 5–18 minutes to discuss the summary question as a group. Designate someone who will summarize the small group discussion and

report to the larger group. Remind the designated person that he/she will only have one minute to present.

C. LARGE GROUP PRESENTATIONS

1. Large Group Leader

Reconvene the Group. Call the groups back to rejoin as a class. If they are in different locations of the building, consider sending a designated person around to each location or selecting another method of notifying them that time is up.

Explain the Procedure. Explain that a representative of each small group will share that group's reflections on the Williams' problem with the larger group. Then the large group, together, can discuss a Ministry Application and reflect together on making a practical application of what has been learned.

Remind Small Group Representatives of the Time. Remind each small group representative that he/she should try to summarize the group's discussion in one minute. Be sure that the small group presenters connect their presentations both to the case study of the Williams' situation and to people with similar problems. During this second session, the presentations should be somewhat easier since most participants will be more familiar with the format than last time. The respective small group emphasis should be on helping people to:

Group #1: Understand the power of God's promises
Group #2: Recognize the rewards of obedience to God's promises
Group #3: Realize the importance of keeping your promises
Group #4: Overcome doubt and unbelief
Group #5: Refute Satan's lies with Scripture

Be sure that they relate some of the Scriptures from the exercises to each of the topics above.

2. Ministry Application

Use the worksheet in the student workbook to guide the students through

a plan to develop a financial education ministry in your church. Suggest ways to get expert help from the membership by soliciting those who have experience in banking, credit counseling, finance, or accounting. Consider the resource book *The Urban Guide to Biblical Money Management,* available from UMI, as a possible study guide for this group.

3. Personal Application

Ask participants, between this session and the next, to think about the Personal Application (exercise #7) and to read chapter three. Call their attention to the study questions at the end of chapter three in the workbook. Encourage them to come to the next session prepared to share insights on their Personal Application of the contents of this chapter.

D. PRAYER

Hold hands and, in a circle, ask for specific prayer requests. Then ask for several volunteers to pray while keeping the prayer requests in mind.

ANSWERS TO BIBLE APPLICATION EXERCISES

1. The Nature of God's Promises

a. All the Lord's promises are true; the Word of the Lord is tried.

b. The Lord's promises are pure.

c. All the Lord's promises prove true.

d. God's promises will be your armour (shield) and your protection (buckler).

e. God publicly proclaims bold promises; He does not speak in secret.

f. SUMMARY ANSWER: God's promises are always kept, have no fine print or hidden provisions, and prove true when examined initially and over time.

2. God's Promises for Those Who Keep His Commands

a. God will keep His promises and show unfailing love or mercy.

b. God will always fulfill His promises.

c. The Scriptures give us hope and encouragement while we wait for God's promises.

d. You will share in God's divine nature and escape the corruption in the world.

e. God will not forsake you; He will not abandon you or destroy you.

f. SUMMARY ANSWER: Keeping the commands of God allows us to claim the benefits of God's promises to believers. God's faithfulness can be counted on. No matter what the circumstances are or how long it seems to take, you can be assured that He will answer and keep His promises to you. These Scriptures can provide the starting point for discussions about this.

3. Keeping Your Promises
a. The Lord is a witness to all our promises.
b. Others are watching and witnessing our promises.
c. We should not make rash promises and should guard our words.
d. It is better to say nothing than to make a promise that you do not keep.
e. God keeps His promises, even when we break ours.
f. SUMMARY ANSWER: Approved credit applications involve promises to pay. Debt is a commitment made to a financial institution, but it is also a commitment that is made before God and His people. We should be careful not to overcommit, and we should also be careful to keep the commitments that we make. The consequences of not keeping our financial commitments can affect our families, our relationships with others, and our relationship with God.

4. The Enemy of God's Promises
a. The enemy is deceptive and will lie about God's promises.
b. The enemy tempts the believer to break commitments to God by targeting the flesh, the things of the world, and pride. He will use partial truth and take God's promises out of context.
c. The enemy actively seeks those who may be susceptible to breaking commitments made to God and others.
d. Unbelief can result in failing to receive the blessings of God.
e. The faithful and the patient inherit the promises of God.
f. SUMMARY ANSWER: The believer should be always sober and watchful, aware that the enemy can be deceptive and is looking for

those who would fall prey to his schemes. Skepticism is a healthy attitude when viewing the ads on television that are all designed to make you want to own and purchase the things advertised. Our focus should remain on the things of God, and we should avoid pursuing promises of this world, materialism, and hedonistic pleasures.

5. The False Promises of the Enemy

a. We should have firm convictions so that the deceitfulness of the enemy does not shift our opinion about what we know to be true.

b. The time will come, and is no doubt now here, when those who would make false promises to the people of God will teach doctrines that appeal to the lusts of men and not the truths of God. This prophetic admonition speaks clearly to a time of false promises from those in ministry who would seek to lead people astray by promising what people want to hear, not what God wants for His people.

c. We should be careful not to be misled by philosophies and deceptive promises that do not line up with the Word of God. Worldly and high-minded statements that are at odds with God's Word can lead to bad decisions and unwise choices. Therefore, we should be on our guard when watching television programs and commercials that make the case for things that are ungodly.

d. The deception of Satan can include unusual and supernatural appearances. The special effects of television can create appearances that are completely false when carefully examined or scrutinized. All types of wicked deception can be used by the enemy in attempts to deceive the believer; those who have not believed are especially vulnerable.

e. It is important that we test what we hear against the Word of God. Falsehood is all around us and everything that sounds good isn't.

f. SUMMARY ANSWER: Television presents many opportunities for deception. The statements made and lifestyles displayed on many programs focus on the wealth and riches of this world; through this medium, the lie is presented that there is a satisfaction in life that can be achieved apart from God.

6. Ministry Application

A clothing bank is a ministry activity that is simple to execute and requires very little resources. Many communities have charities that are already established to retrieve and distribute clothing that is collected. A commitment should be made to include new as well as used clothing and shoes. During the winter months, coats are always a needed item in colder climates and the need for children's clothing can be critical, given that the majority of African American children are being raised in single parent homes where finances are often limited.

CHAPTER THREE

TELEVISION–
Miracles and Ministry

Format for Sessions of 90 Minutes or More

PART ONE		PART TWO*	
MIN.	ACTIVITY	MIN.	ACTIVITY
5	Prayer	5	Case Study
10	Introduction	30	Small Group Study
15	Scripture Discussion	10	Small Group Presentations
10	Chapter Highlights	18	Large Group Discussion
		3	Prayer

*For sessions of less than 90 minutes, use PART ONE only, and assign the case study as homework. *To complete the activities in PART TWO, each participant will need the workbook that accompanies the student book.*

LESSON AIM: At the end of this two–part training session, the participant should be able to: a) describe several healing miracles recorded in the Old Testament and New Testament; b) explain one or more of Jesus' teachings on healing; c) explain several spiritual principles concerning healing.

I. PART ONE

A. PRAYER

Open the session with prayer while keeping the lesson aim in mind.

B. PERSONAL REFLECTIONS

Last time, participants were asked to make personal applications of the material covered in the last session, using exercise #7 of chapter two. Allow time for volunteers to share the results of this Personal Application. Then introduce the lesson for today—Miracles and Ministry.

C. SCRIPTURE DISCUSSION

Read Luke 2:49; Mark 5:22–42; and Acts 10:38. Alternate between leader and group. Then discuss the following questions:

1. Why was healing important in the ministry of Jesus?
2. What are some of the different ways that healing took place?
3. What were some of the actions taken by those who were healed?
4. Why did Jesus put the mourners out at the death of Jairus's daughter?
5. What was the source of Jesus' power to heal?

D. CHAPTER HIGHLIGHTS

Explain that the chapter focuses the power of God manifested in the healing miracles of Jesus and the healing ministries we sometimes see on television. A review of the healing ministries of Jesus in Mark 5 is contrasted with the way that healing is presented by television ministries today. Using chapter three as background, provide a general overview of the points made in the chapter. Be sure to discuss the following questions:

1. What is the relationship between Jesus' healing power and the proof of His deity?
2. Who reached out for healing, and what was Jesus' response?
3. How have television special effects changed our perception of miracles?
4. What are some criticisms of religious television?
5. According to the study mentioned in the chapter, what kinds of people are most likely to give to television ministries?

6. How can television ministries be more effective in demonstrating the power of God?

Ask the group to reflect for a few minutes on fraud in television ministries. Has there been lasting damage to the church from fraudulent televangelism? Is the power of the miraculous available to the church today?

II. PART TWO

To complete the activities in PART TWO, participants will need the workbooks that accompany the student books.

A. CASE STUDY
1. Introduction
Explain that the case study in the workbook is an opportunity to apply the principles presented in the chapter to a real–life story. Reverend Charles, in the case study, has decided to move his ministry into television.

2. Procedure
Select Small Group Leaders. Ask for volunteers or select five group leaders. Then assign each group leader a number (1–5). (This can be done beforehand.) Ask each group leader to write their number on a large sheet of paper so that it can be seen from a distance.

Divide into Small Groups. Inform them that they will be forming five small groups. Each group will study a different set of questions related to the chapter and will present their findings to the larger group at the end of the small group study period. The set of questions to be studied should correspond with the numbers of the groups as follows:

Group #1: Old Testament Miracles of Healing
Group #2: New Testament Miracles of Healing
Group #3: Jesus Confronts the Pharisees' Objections About Healing
Group #4: Will Everyone Be Healed?
Group #5: Healing and Television Ministries

Have the participants count off by fives. Then have them join the small group leader that is displaying their respective assigned number. Inform them of the meeting places for each of the groups. (These locations can be printed beforehand to facilitate a smoother transition.) Then allow the participants to assemble into the smaller groups at their designated meeting places.

B. SMALL GROUP STUDY

1. Small Group Leaders Allocate Questions

For each exercise, there are five "discovery" questions and a summary question. Therefore, each small group will have one exercise to complete, and that exercise will involve answering five questions and a summary question. Assign one discovery question to each person in the group. If there are more people than questions, allow people to work on questions in twos or threes, etc. If there are less people than questions, assign more than one question per person.

Don't consider the summary question at this time. The small group will discuss it at the end of the small group study time, and it will be used as a basis for the small group's presentation to the larger group. Ask each person (or pair, etc.) to answer the assigned question.

2. Share Insights

After 10 minutes, ask the small group participants to come together in their groups. Allow each one to tell the question that he/she had and his/her answer to it. Then allow 5–18 minutes to discuss the summary question as a group. Designate someone who will summarize the small group discussion and report to the larger group. Remind the designated person that he/she will only have one minute to present.

C. LARGE GROUP PRESENTATIONS

1. Large Group Leader

Reconvene the Group. Call the small groups back together. If they are in different locations of the building, consider sending a designated person around to each location or selecting another method of notifying them that time is up.

Explain the Procedure. Explain that a representative of each small group will share that group's reflections on healing and miracles. When the large group comes together, they can discuss the Ministry Application and reflect on making a practical application of what has been learned.

Remind Small Group Representatives of the Time. Remind each small group representative that he/she should try to summarize their group's discussion in one minute. Be sure that the small group presenters connect their presentations both to the case study and to the Scripture's teachings on Jesus' miraculous healings. The respective small group emphasis should be on:

Group #1: Understanding the relationship between prayer, obedience, and healing

Group #2: How Jesus validated His ministry through healing miracles

Group #3: The challenges given to Jesus by the Pharisees

Group #4: If there are limits to healing

Group #5: Miracles and the church today

Be sure that they relate some of the Scriptures from the exercises to each of the topics above.

2. Ministry Application

Ask them to divide into five groups. Ask each group to attempt a unique approach to exercise #6 in the workbook. Call their attention to the worksheet that can be used for this purpose.

3. Personal Application

Allow about 15 minutes for them to complete the assigned question. Then reconvene the group and ask them to present the outcomes of their discussions.

D. PRAYER

Hold hands and, in a circle, ask for specific prayer requests. Then ask for several volunteers to pray while keeping the prayer requests in mind.

ANSWERS TO BIBLE APPLICATION EXERCISES

1. Old Testament Miracles of Healing

a. Elijah raises a widow woman's son from the dead.

b. Elisha heals Naaman of leprosy after his wife's maid tells of Elisha's ministry.

c. Job is healed from a personal tragedy including loss of family members and wealth.

d. Nebuchadnezzar loses his sanity and his kingdom, but God restores them both when he acknowledges God's greatness and power.

e. After finding out about his fatal illness from Isaiah, Hezekiah prays and God extends his life by 15 years.

f. SUMMARY ANSWER: Healing occurred when it was sought through prayer and through obedience to the instructions of the man of God.

2. New Testament Miracles of Healing

a. Jesus heals a leper and then instructs him to go to the priests and show himself as a testimony to them.

b. Jesus heals two blind men and then instructs them to tell no one, but they spread the word throughout the countryside.

c. Jesus heals a deaf and dumb man that was brought to Him by a crowd of people.

d. Jesus heals a cripple who had been at the pool at Bethesda. The man had been crippled for 38 years.

e. Peter's mother-in-law is healed and arises to serve Jesus and the other guests at her house.

f. SUMMARY ANSWER: Jesus' healings were not limited to age, condition, or time. He healed the young and the old, the crippled, the deaf, dumb, and blind. There are no limits on God's power.

3. Jesus Confronts the Pharisees' Objections About Healing

a. Jesus challenged the Pharisees with a question designed to show that spirit of the law was more important than the letter of the law as they interpreted it. He heals a man on the Sabbath in the synagogue, both demonstrating His power and presenting a new interpretation of the law that it was lawful to do good on the Sabbath.

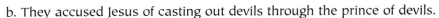

b. They accused Jesus of casting out devils through the prince of devils.

c. Jesus presents three arguments: 1) that if He healed by the power of Satan, then Satan's kingdom was divided against itself since it would be undoing damage it had done; 2) that the Pharisees also healed, so by what power did they heal?; 3) that it is only by binding a strong man that you can overcome his power. Jesus must have overcome the power of Satan to accomplish the healings.

d. Jesus had healed on the Sabbath; to the Pharisees, this violation of the law made Jesus a sinner, but they could not understand how a sinner could perform miracles.

e. Jesus described them as spiritually blind since they could not see His deity; yet the Pharisees thought they had spiritual insight and wisdom.

f. SUMMARY ANSWER: There are often disagreements about who really represents God and who is authentic. The demonstrated power of God through actual results could be more significant than power or position in a religious institution. (There may be other answers.)

4. Will Everyone Be Healed?

a. David prayed and fasted and sought the Lord for the healing of his child.

b. When David realized that his child had died, he cleaned himself up and worshiped God. He acknowledged that the outcome was God's will and then accepted God's response.

c. Jesus said that the disciples were unable to heal in this instance because of their unbelief. He then added that this particular demon only responded to prayer and fasting.

d. Paul said that eating and drinking at a celebration of the Lord's Supper unworthily has caused some to become sick, weak, or even die.

e. James instructed the sick to call for the elders of the church to let them pray and anoint the sick with oil in the name of the Lord.

f. SUMMARY ANSWER: God's Word does not change. The wisdom and truth of Scripture regarding disease and illness stands with all other teachings of the Bible.

5. Healing and Television Ministries

a. Television provides outreach that could help Christians obey the command of Jesus to "go and teach all nations" (Matthew 28:19). Television could be used to minister to those who are unable to come to worship services. Other answers are possible.

b. Reverend Charles' book could have been used as a study guide or reference for a teaching series on healing. Depending on the content, it may have been useful as a supplement to his preaching or teaching on the television program. Bible study is encouraged in several Scriptures, such as 2 Timothy 2:15; 3:15–16.

c. Money given to this ministry could be used to advance the television ministry or to advance the ministry of the local church, depending on the mission and ministry of the church. The use of all resources should ultimately advance the kingdom of God and not be directed toward turning the ministry into a kingdom.

d. Television could be considered as a medium for outreach. Some feel that outreach involves personal contact with those who need Christ and requires the support of the local church personally engaged in the lives of others.

e. Ministry growth can be seen in increased numbers or in the development of a deeper relationship with Christ in those who are currently involved.

f. SUMMARY ANSWER: Whatever is done should be done to the glory of God and not to take advantage of the condition of those who seek healing.

6. Ministry Application

Discuss students' plans and how to implement them.

CHAPTER FOUR

TELEVISION—
Salvation and Love

Format for Sessions of 90 Minutes or More

PART ONE		PART TWO*	
MIN.	ACTIVITY	MIN.	ACTIVITY
5	Prayer	5	Case Study
10	Personal Reflections	30	Small Group Study
15	Scripture Discussion	10	Small Group Presentations
10	Chapter Highlights	18	Large Group Discussion
		3	Prayer

*For sessions of less than 90 minutes, use PART ONE only, and assign the case study as homework. *To complete the PART TWO activities, each participant will need the workbook that accompanies the student book.*

LESSON AIM: At the end of this two–part training session, the participant should be able to: a) give a definition of God's love; b) identify ways parents can help their children understand love and build true love relationships; c) explain the risks and problems that result from the love of power; d) identify the three major areas of temptation for believers; e) describe the attributes of the love of God as shown in salvation.

I. PART ONE

A. PRAYER

Consider opening with a hymn or song about love, such as "Oh How I Love Jesus." Open the session with prayer while keeping the lesson aim in mind.

B. PERSONAL REFLECTIONS

Last time, participants were asked to make personal applications of the material covered in the last session, using exercise #7 of chapter three. Allow time for volunteers to share the results of this personal application. Then introduce the lesson for today—Salvation and Love.

C. SCRIPTURE DISCUSSION

Read Romans 5:1–8; Romans 10:9; and 1 John 1:9. Alternate between leader and group. Then discuss the following questions:

1. How does man's sinful condition provide an opportunity for God's love?
2. Who or what would you die for?
3. What does a person have to do to be saved?
4. How does God deal with sin after we are saved?

D. CHAPTER HIGHLIGHTS

Explain that the chapter focuses on how television distorts love and reinforces the world's versions of love. Review the three lusts of the flesh: power, money, and the things it can buy. Identify and briefly discuss television shows that illustrate these lusts as their major themes. Get the group to discuss the differences between the love of God and the lusts of the world as seen on television. Be sure to review how God's love, not our behavior or works, provides salvation. Be sure to include the following questions:

1. What is love?
2. What are the different types of love?

3. How is love shown on television, and what is the major expression of love on TV?
4. How does television teach children to love money and power?
5. How does 1 Corinthians 13 describe love?
6. Why does associating good works with salvation lead to uncertainty about being saved?
7. How does God provide for forgiveness of sin committed after a person has received salvation?

Discuss how love develops in relationships and what happens over time. Provide enough time for participants to explore different situations and discuss how the principles presented in the chapter and the Bible study might apply to them.

II. PART TWO

To complete the activities in PART TWO, each participant will need the workbook that accompanies the student book.

A. CASE STUDY

1. Introduction
Explain that the case study in the workbook provides an opportunity to apply the principles presented in the chapter to a real-life story. Ask the group to reflect on Justin and Andrette's situation from the workbook case study. Encourage people who may have experienced this type of situation to share their experiences. Look to find perspectives from both parents and those who may themselves have been faced with an out-of-wedlock pregnancy.

2. Procedure
Select Small Group Leaders. Ask for volunteers or select five group leaders. Then assign each small group leader a number (1–5.) If paper is unavailable, ask the leaders to stand in different sections of the room so that participants can easily identify them.

Divide into Small Groups. Inform the participants that they will be forming five small groups. Each group will study a different set of questions related to the case study and will present their findings to the larger group at the end of the small group study period. The set of questions to be studied should correspond with the group numbers as follows:

Group #1: The Bible's Definition of Love

Group #2: The Role of Parental Love

Group #3: Love and Power

Group #4: Love Versus Lust

Group #5: The Love of God

Ask the class (excluding the group leaders) to count off by fives. Discourage the formation of permanent groups. That is, many participants may be gravitating toward the same group each session and come to class with the same people. Therefore, they may be highly likely to interact with most of the same people in their groups each week. To avoid this, tell them that it is a good idea to meet and interact with new people. Then tell them that to facilitate this, you will begin the counting from a different point in the room, thus making it unlikely that identical groups will be formed each session. Ask them to join the small group leader that is displaying their respective number. Inform them of the meeting places for each of the groups. (These locations can be printed beforehand, to facilitate a smoother transition.) Then allow the participants to assemble into the smaller groups at their designated meeting places.

B. SMALL GROUP STUDY

1. Small Group Leaders Allocate Questions

For each exercise, there are five "discovery" questions and a summary question. Therefore, each small group will have one exercise to complete, and that exercise will involve answering five questions and a summary question.

Assign one discovery question to each person in the group. If there are more people than questions allow people to work on questions in twos or threes, etc. If there are more questions than people, assign more than one

question per person. Don't consider the summary question at this time. The small group will discuss it at the end of group study time, and it will be used as a basis for the small group's presentation to the larger group. Ask each person (or pair, etc.) to answer the assigned question.

2. Share Insights

After 10 minutes, ask the small group participants to come together in their groups. Allow each to tell the question that he/she had and his/her answer to it. Allow 5–18 minutes to discuss the summary question as a group. Then designate someone who will summarize the small group discussion and report to the larger group. Remind the designated person that he/she will only have one minute to present.

C. LARGE GROUP PRESENTATIONS

1. Large Group Leader

Reconvene the Group. If the small groups are in different locations of the building, consider sending a designated person around to each location or selecting another method of notifying them that time is up.

Explain the Procedure. Explain that a representative of each small group will share that group's reflections on different types of love with the larger group. Then the large group, together, can discuss the Ministry Application and reflect on making a practical application of what has been learned.

Remind Small Group Representatives of the Time. Remind each small group representative that he/she should try to summarize the group's discussion in one minute. Be sure that the small group presenters connect their small group presentations to the case study of Justin and Andrette and the Bible's examples of love. The respective small group emphasis should be on:

Group #1: The biblical definitions of love as described in 1 Corinthians 13 and love as illustrated in the life of Christ and some of the relationships of Joseph and David

Group #2: The role of parents and in-laws in shaping love relationships according to the stories of Rebecca, Ruth, and the guidance from Proverbs

Group #3: The often disastrous consequences of the quest for and love of power

Group #4: The three areas of sin and lusts that plague believers

Group #5: The love of God and how God's love responds

Be sure that they relate some of the Scriptures from the exercises to each of the topics above.

2. Ministry Application

Use the worksheet in the workbook as a guide for helping the group to design a church-based ministry that addresses one of the outreach opportunities listed. If time permits, allow them to divide into small groups and brainstorm while completing one worksheet for each group. Then ask them to share their designs with the larger group.

3. Personal Application

Call their attention to the section set aside for journalizing in their workbooks. Ask them to reflect on the Personal Application (exercise #7) between this session and the next, and to use the journalizing section to write down their thoughts. They should also read chapter five in the student book, and reflect on the questions at the end of the chapter in preparation for the next session.

D. PRAYER

Hold hands and, in a circle, ask for specific prayer requests. Then ask for several volunteers to pray while keeping the prayer requests in mind.

ANSWERS TO BIBLE APPLICATION EXERCISES

1. The Bible's Definition of Love

a. Justin found himself in continual close contact with a female who was not his wife, but, unlike Joseph, he created the opportunity for temptation. Potiphar's wife had a physical (erotic love) attraction for Joseph just as Justin was probably more physically attracted to Andrette than anything else.

b. Like David and Jonathan, Andrette and Justin were friends who had family relationships and spent lots of time together. David and Jonathan were committed to each other as brothers and loved each other in that way, while Justin and Andrette were potentially looking to develop a deeper love as a married couple.

c. Both Justin and David were godly men who allowed themselves to be subject to physical temptation. Neither intended to cause a pregnancy or get married. Justin appears ready to admit to his sin, while Davis tried to cover his.

d. Patience, kindness, modesty, humility, graciousness, and other attributes.

e. God's love for man was so great that he sacrificed His only Son to save us from our sins.

f. SUMMARY ANSWER: Love should be based on the principles of 1 Corinthians 13 and the self-sacrificing example of Jesus Christ. Distinguish other types of "love."

2. The Role of Parental Love

a. Rebekah and Isaac decided on the family and ethnicity of their son's spouse by sending him to another region with specific instructions on which family to marry into. They decided that, unlike his brother, he should not marry the women in the region where they lived.

b. Naomi gave Ruth explicit instructions about where to go, what to wear, what to do, and how to groom herself to best meet the man she ultimately married.

c. No matter what their views are on whether their children should marry or not, they should respond to them in love (see Galatians 6:1; Ephesians 6:4; and Proverbs 10:12).

d. Yes, child training in relationship skills are most critical. Proverbs 22:6 covers all child training.

e. They should be prepared to love them unconditionally, help and encourage them to complete their education, and be prepared to assist in the rearing of the grandchild (see Deuteronomy 6:7; Ephesians 6:4; and 1 Timothy 1:5).

f. SUMMARY ANSWER: The parents appear to have routinely left their children at home, alone and unsupervised, and allowed them to have company during times when they were not around. It is possible that the parents failed to model good relationship skills. Justin's father may have inadvertently encouraged promiscuity in his son by his comments. The parents may have focused more on church attendance than actual relationship with Jesus Christ. (There are no absolute right or wrong answers since the case is ambiguous on these points. Be sure that answers include stated assumptions where no information is given or the facts are unclear.)

3. Love and Power

a. When working together in unity is combined with man's love of power, it makes virtually nothing impossible.

b. Whoever exalts himself above God or seeks equality with God will be brought down.

c. He may have been using his relationship as a means to achieve his quest for power and position.

d. In the end, all manipulation is destructive. Both Jezebel and Ahab were destroyed and brought ruin to their families because of power-grabbing, manipulative behavior.

e. Satan offered Jesus power over all the world's kingdoms if Jesus would bow down and worship him.

f. SUMMARY ANSWER: Power and position present great temptations that should be avoided. Men and women should especially be on guard against any goal for power or position that requires an ungodly relationship to achieve it. Manipulation of people should not be an end of a love relationship. Love always views the other person as a ministry, not as a means to an end. With regard to power, Jesus said that we should seek first the kingdom (Matthew 6:33).

4. Love Versus Lust

a. The lust of the flesh, the lust of the eyes, and the pride of life are the three areas of temptation. Jesus was tempted in His fleshly hunger to turn stones to bread, by the sight of Satan's offer of the world's kingdoms, and by the temptation to proudly test God's divine protection of Him.

b. Justin was tempted by his physical desire to engage in sex outside of marriage. He may also have been tempted by his pride to be in a position of student leadership. He should have responded by relying on the Word of God to help him overcome the temptation (Psalms 119:11; 1 Corinthians 6:18).

c. Justin was older and could have been exposed to more biblical teaching as a pastor's child. He also could have been a target for Satan because of his position in the church.

d. Jesus' attitude toward sexual impurity is that it begins in the heart. He teaches that looking on a woman with lust is the beginning of the sin.

e. The psalmist commits to put nothing vile before his eyes. We should avoid watching anything that tempts us to lust, including television, the Internet, movies, magazines, or any other vile vision.

f. SUMMARY ANSWER: Teach your children that temptation will come in the flesh (physical desires), in pride, and in the desire for the things of the world (1 John 1:16). Encourage memorization of key Scripture verses that will provide a "way of escape" (1 Corinthians 10:13). Use common sense and do not open your home to situations where the opportunity for lust and sin can overcome children.

5. The Love of God

a. God's response to us is love: "But commended his love toward us, in that, while we were yet sinners Christ died for us" (Romans 5:8).

b. First John 1:9 says that God will forgive our sins if we confess them.

c. Both Justin and Andrette seemed to think that their church activities and involvement should have assured them special protections from

God. God's love does not depend on our works, and our works do not assure God's love.

d. Husbands are told to love their wives like Christ loved the church.

e. This relationship does not show us God. God is love and would not fornicate.

f. SUMMARY ANSWER: Their parents should seek to love them in spite of their mistakes, encourage them to repent so that they can be in right relationship with God, and pray with them that sin will not prevent them from reflecting God's love to others.

6. Ministry Application

Some ministries have focused all their outreach efforts on those who most need God's love. However, the poor, the homeless, the widowed, and orphans are often overlooked in the development of ministries. Consider how much effort goes into loving those inside your church as compared to those outside.

CHAPTER FIVE

TELEVISION—
Christianity and Food

Format for Sessions of 90 Minutes or More

PART ONE		PART TWO*	
MIN.	ACTIVITY	MIN.	ACTIVITY
5	Prayer	5	Case Study
10	Personal Reflections	30	Small Group Study
15	Scripture Discussion	10	Small Group Presentations
10	Chapter Highlights	18	Large Group Discussion
		3	Prayer

*For sessions of less than 90 minutes, use PART ONE only, and assign the case study as homework. *To complete the activities in PART TWO, each participant will need the workbook that accompanies the student book.*

LESSON AIM: At the end of this two–part training session, the participant should be able to: a) understand how God feeds and cares for those who serve Him; b) understand the biblical support for providing provision for those in church leadership; c) discuss the contradiction in U.S. food supply being so large while many still go hungry; d) explain how televi-

sion contributes to poor dietary practices; e) discuss the health risks of physical inactivity and obesity; f) identify the connection between passive television watching and obesity.

I. PART ONE

A. PRAYER
Open the session with prayer, including the lesson aim.

B. PERSONAL REFLECTIONS
Participants were asked to make personal applications of the material covered in the last session, using exercise #7 of chapter four. Allow time for volunteers to share the results of this Personal Application. Then introduce the lesson for today—Christianity and Food.

C. SCRIPTURE DISCUSSION
Read 1 Kings 17:1–16. Alternate between leader and group. Then discuss the following questions:
1. What was the command of God to Elijah?
2. How did God use the ravens, and how did they fulfill their responsibility?
3. How did God use the widow at Zarephath?
4. What was the result of the widow's obedience?

D. CHAPTER HIGHLIGHTS
Explain that the chapter focuses on God's provision of food and sustenance for those in leadership and the state of television, the food business, hunger, and obesity in the U.S. today. The contradiction between obesity and hunger is explored and a connection is made between obesity and the physical inactivity that results from television watching. Using chapter five as background, provide a general overview of the points made in the chapter. Be sure to raise the following questions:
1. Why is it important to provide for those in ministry?

2. What is the purpose of provision for those in leadership?
3. What are some of the current problems with the food business in the U.S.?
4. How are disease and death related to poor eating habits?
5. What are some advertising strategies used on television that contribute to poor eating habits?
6. What are some practical ways of dealing with poor dietary practices and their consequences?

Ask the group to reflect on Sister Johnson's situation (from the workbook case study). Guide them in exploring the situation. Ask what they feel are some of the reasons this situation could have occurred. How can old habits and behaviors be changed? What are some of the challenges in working with senior adults who have to effect lifestyle changes that may be difficult? What other approaches could have been considered to encourage her husband to seek regular medical care?

II. PART TWO

To complete the PART TWO activities, each participant will need the workbook that accompanies the student book.

A. CASE STUDY

1. Introduction
Explain that the case study is an opportunity to apply the principles presented in the chapter to a real–life story. Sister Johnson has to completely change her approach to meal preparation and food to accommodate the dietary restrictions of a newly diagnosed medical condition. Failure to effectively comply could have serious consequences for her and her husband.

2. Procedure
Select Small Group Leaders. Ask for volunteers or select five group leaders. Then assign each group leader a number (1–5). (This can be done before-

hand.) Ask each group leader to write their number on a large sheet of paper so that they can easily be seen.

Divide into Small Groups. Inform the participants that they will be forming five small groups. Each group will study a different set of questions related to the case study and will present their findings to the larger group at the end of the group study period. The set of questions to be studied should correspond with the group numbers as follows:

Group #1: God's Provision for His People
Group #2: God's Provision for His Servants
Group #3: New Testament Teachings on Food and Provision
Group #4: Feeding Those in Need
Group #5: Food and Care of the Temple (the Body)

Have the participants count off by fives. Then ask them to join the small group leader that is displaying their respective assigned number. Inform them of the meeting places for each of the group. (These locations can also be printed beforehand to facilitate a smoother transition.) Then allow the participants to assemble into the small groups at their designated meeting places.

B. SMALL GROUP STUDY
1. Small Group Leaders Allocate Questions

For each exercise, there are five "discovery" questions and a summary question. Therefore, each small group will have one exercise to complete, and that exercise will involve answering five questions and a summary question.

Assign one discovery question to each person. If there are more people than questions, allow people to work on questions in twos or threes, etc. If there are less people than questions, assign more than one question per person. Don't consider the summary question at this time; the small group will discuss it at the end of the group study time, and it will be used as a basis for the small group's presentation to the larger group. Ask each person (or pair, etc.) to answer the assigned question.

2. Share Insights

After 10 minutes, ask the small group participants to come together in their groups. Allow each one to tell the question that he/she had and his/her answer to it. Then allow 5–18 minutes to discuss the summary question as a group. Designate someone who will summarize the small group discussion and report to the larger group. Remind the designated person that he/she will only have one minute to present.

C. LARGE GROUP PRESENTATIONS

1. Large Group Leader

Reconvene the Group. Call the small groups back together. If they are in different locations of the building, consider sending someone to each location or selecting another method of notifying them that time is up.

Explain the Procedure. Explain that a representative of each small group will share that group's reflections on provision with the larger group. Then the large group, together, can discuss a final summary exercise and reflect on making a practical application of what has been learned.

Remind Small Group Representatives of the Time. Remind each small group representative that they should try to summarize their group's discussion in one minute.

Be sure that the small group presenters connect their presentations both to the case study of Sister Johnson and to people with similar marital, health, parental, and dietary problems. The respective small group emphasis should be on:

Group #1: How God provides for His people
Group #2: How God provides for His servants
Group #3: What the New Testament teaches about food and provision
Group #4: Our responsibility to feed those in need
Group #5: Taking care of our temples

Be sure that they relate some of the Scriptures from the exercises to each of the topics above.

2. Ministry Application

Lead participants through the development of a food ministry team to help members of a local community who are food insecure—people who are regularly without adequate resources to provide healthy meals for themselves and their families. If possible, write the headings of the three columns on a chalkboard or newsprint. If an overhead projector and overhead transparency film are available, the headings can be presented in this manner.

3. Personal Application

Ask them, between this session and the next, to reflect on the Personal Application (exercise #7) and to read chapter six.

D. PRAYER

Hold hands and, in a circle, ask for specific prayer requests. Then ask for several volunteers to pray, keeping the prayer requests in mind.

ANSWERS TO BIBLE APPLICATION EXERCISES

1. God's Provision for His People

a. God planted a garden for food for Adam, the first man.

b. God gave Joseph a plan to store grain for seven years in anticipation of a famine. Joseph stored food and later was able to sell food to other countries because of the severity of the famine.

c. The Lord provided quail in the evening and bread (manna) in the morning for them to eat.

d. God provided food for the poor by decreeing that fields were not to be stripped clean at harvest but rather that the edges would be left for the poor to glean from.

e. The priests were allowed to eat from the offerings that had been brought for sacrifices in the evening after they had washed themselves.

f. SUMMARY ANSWER: God will provide food for His people and use His people to provide food for others.

2. God's Provision for His Servants

a. Jesus instructed them to not take money or extra clothing and to depend on the people being ministered to for support.

b. One who receives a prophet will receive a prophet's reward.

c. Ministers have the right to eat just as others, soldiers do not serve at their own expense, and shepherds drink the milk of the flocks they tend. Paul also gives a basis for support from the Law of Moses (Deuteronomy 25:4).

d. Elders should be treated with "double honor."

e. God says He will hold such leaders accountable and remove them.

f. SUMMARY ANSWER: Many churches today probably more than adequately meet the standards of provision for pastors. Some provide more and others provide less, but most controversy today seems to focus on how much provision is enough, not issues of too little provision.

3. New Testament Teachings on Food and Provision

a. Jesus said that life is more important than food and the body more important than clothes.

b. The body and the life in it are the temple that God dwells in to carry out the work in this world; the presence of God that can only be accomplished through believers yielded to His will.

c. Jesus told us to seek God's kingdom and His righteousness first, and then all these other things will be given to us.

d. In these Scriptures, Jesus takes the food that was available, a few loaves of bread and a few pieces of fish, and feeds thousands of people. This miracle dramatically demonstrated God's ability to provide food for His followers and the power of Jesus in provision.

e. Jesus made it clear that the Pharisees' traditions of ceremonial washing was not at the core of God's laws about food and eating. But rather, God was concerned about the condition of the heart and the thoughts of man.

f. SUMMARY ANSWER: Sister Johnson could use the times she shares with her daughter to share Bible stories and teachings that point to

God's concern about the spiritual condition over the physical condition. She could share how, although it is important that her health be maintained, it is more important that she use her good health to further the kingdom of God. Church attendance may have been a family tradition, but the spiritual transformation that should result is what God seeks.

4. Feeding Those in Need

a. The greatest commandment is to love God with all your heart, soul, and mind and to love your neighbor. Providing food is a fundamental expression of love for your neighbor.

b. This passage might be interpreted to mean that Jesus viewed the feeding of the hungry to be the same as feeding or showing mercy to Him.

c. The promise is that those good deeds will never be forgotten (see Psalms 112:9).

d. This passage also establishes the basis for provision for those in ministry and it gives guidance that those who do not work should not eat. Help should be provided for those who truly need help, not for those who are lazy.

e. Don't just talk; take action! Work with agencies that prequalify those who need assistance; use questionnaires or interviews to get the right information to determine the need; or take the ministry to local food pantries or others who screen for need. Some element of evaluation or screening may be needed to assure good stewardship of ministry resources. There may be other answers.

f. SUMMARY ANSWER: Assess the spiritual gifts of those in the fellowship (Acts 6:2–3); choose people who are both wise and spirit–filled (v. 3); delegate full responsibility to them (v. 3); and commission them with prayer and the laying on of hands (v. 6)

5. Food and Care of the Temple (the Body)

a. Your body is the temple of the Holy Spirit and belongs to God.

b. The law says not to eat anything that is detestable (abominable).

c. Gluttony (overeating) produces poverty and destitution.

d. Eglon, the Moabite king, was so fat that he was secretly assassinated by Ehud, the Israelite. Ehud used a knife and thrust it in him so that Eglon's fat covered it.

e. Using the example of athletes in training, Paul relates the importance of having physical discipline as an assurance that our spiritual goals will not become hindered by an undisciplined body.

f. SUMMARY ANSWER: While it is important to distinguish between the value of physical exercise and training as compared to spiritual development, Sister Johnson may not be able to continue her spiritual development if improper diet and lack of exercise causes her health to fail prematurely.

6. Ministry Application

There are no definite answers. The items entered in each column will vary considerably according to the participants.

CHAPTER SIX

TELEVISION–
Violence and God's Protection

Format for Sessions of 90 Minutes or More

PART ONE		PART TWO*	
MIN.	ACTIVITY	MIN.	ACTIVITY
5	Prayer	5	Case Study
10	Personal Reflections	30	Small Group Study
15	Scripture Discussion	10	Small Group Presentations
10	Chapter Highlights	18	Large Group Discussion
		3	Prayer

*For sessions of less than 90 minutes, use PART ONE only, and assign the case study as homework. *For PART TWO activities, participants will need the workbook that accompanies the student book.*

LESSON AIM: At the end of this two–part training session, the participant should be able to: a) explain the significance of Jacob's encounter with God; b) understand the reasons for Jacob's trip to Haran; c) discuss the reasons for fear of death; d) explain the way television teaches fear of death and how to over come this; e) understand the nature and problems of violence on television.

I. PART ONE

A. PRAYER

Distribute index cards and ask each person to write his/her prayer requests on a card. Then ask them to drop the cards in a container such as a tray or brown bag, etc. During prayer time at the end of the session, each person will be asked to take one of the cards and frame a short prayer around it.

B. PERSONAL REFLECTIONS

Allow time for volunteers to share the results of this personal application from their journals in the workbook. Then introduce the lesson for today—Violence and God's Protection.

C. SCRIPTURE DISCUSSION

Read Genesis 28:10–21. Alternate between leader and group. Then discuss the following questions:
1. Why was Jacob going to Haran?
2. What was the promise God made to Jacob?
3. What was the promise made to the rest of the people of the earth?
4. Why was Jacob afraid?
5. What did Jacob do to commemorate the place and the event he experienced?

D. CHAPTER HIGHLIGHTS

Explain that the chapter focuses on God's protection, and death and violence in the media. Ask them to share any instances where they experienced an encounter with the presence of God. What was their response? What should be the Christian's response to death? How have death and violence become subjects for entertainment on television? What is the impact of television violence? How should Christians respond to television violence? Then, using chapter six as background, provide a general overview of the points made in the chapter. Be sure to discuss the following questions:
1. What are the biblical attitudes toward death that believers should hold?

2. How has television violence increased and what has been the impact on society?
3. Which action steps can be taken to address violence on television?

Ask the group to reflect, for a few minutes, on the situation presented in the workbook case study. Ask whether they remember the Columbine shootings, and how they felt when it occurred. Discuss violence in our schools and in our society in general. Provide some time to explore these situations, and discuss how the guidelines presented in the chapter might apply to them.

II. PART TWO

To complete the activities in PART TWO, each participant will need the workbook that accompanies the student book.

A. CASE STUDY
1. Introduction
Explain that the case study in the workbook provides an opportunity to apply the principles presented in the chapter to a real–life story. The case study recounts the Columbine shootings and the testimonies of some who died in this incident after confessing faith in Christ. After reading the case study, ask how the participants believe they would respond if facing certain death for professing their faith.

2. Procedure
Select Small Group Leaders. Ask for volunteers or select five group leaders. Ask them to select numbers, one through five. (This can also be done beforehand.) Ask each leader to write their number on a large sheet of paper so that it can easily be seen.

Divide into Small Groups. Inform the participants that they will divide into five small groups. Each group will study a different set of questions related to the case study and will present their findings to the larger group at the end of

the small group study period. Have the participants count off by fives. Ask them to join the small group leader that is displaying their respective assigned number. Inform them of the meeting places for each of the groups. (These locations can be printed beforehand to facilitate a smoother transition.) Then allow the participants to assemble into the smaller groups at their designated meeting places.

B. SMALL GROUP STUDY

1. Small Group Leaders Allocate Questions

For each exercise, there are five "discovery" questions and a summary question. Therefore, each small group will have one exercise to complete, and that exercise will involve answering five questions and a summary question.

Assign one discovery question to each person in the group. If there are more people than questions, allow people to work on questions in twos or threes, etc. If there are more questions than people, assign more than one question per person. Don't consider the summary question at this time; the small group will discuss it at the end of the group study time, and it will be used as a basis for the small group's presentation to the larger group. Ask each person (or pair, etc.) to answer the assigned question.

2. Share Insights

After 10 minutes, ask the small group participants to come together in their groups. Allow each to tell the question that he/she had and his/her answer to it. Then allow 5–18 minutes to discuss the summary question as a group. Designate someone to summarize the small group discussion and report to the larger group. Remind the designated person that he/she will only have one minute to present.

C. LARGE GROUP PRESENTATIONS

1. Large Group Leader

Reconvene the Group. Call the small groups back together. If they are in different locations of the building, consider sending a designated person to each location or selecting another method of notifying them to reconvene.

Explain the Procedure. Explain that a representative of each small group

will share that group's reflections on the Columbine shootings and God's response to violence with the larger group. Then the large group, together, can discuss the Ministry Application found in the workbook.

Remind Small Group Representatives of the Time. Remind each small group representative that he/she should try to summarize the group's discussion in one minute. Be sure that the small group presenters connect their small group presentations both to the case study of Columbine and to other situations where violence has occurred. By now, most will be accustomed to the format. The respective small group emphasis should be on:
Group #1: God's Presence Revealed
Group #2: God's Protection from Violence in the Old Testament
Group #3: God's Protection from Violence in the New Testament
Group #4: God's Response to Violent Living
Group #5: Violence and Life in the Spirit

Be sure that they relate some of the Scriptures from the exercises to each of the topics above.

2. Ministry Application
The purpose of this exercise is to discover how principles discussed in the chapter can be used within a local church–based ministry and in the outreach ministries of the local church.

3. Personal Application
Call their attention to the section in chapter six of the workbook, which is set aside for journalizing. Ask them to use it, between this session and the next, to write down their responses to exercise #7. They are also to read chapter seven in the student book and reflect on the questions in preparation for the next session.

D. PRAYER
Have everyone get in a circle. After shuffling the index cards that were placed in the container at the beginning of the session, pass around the con-

tainer and ask each person to draw an index card from it. Then ask each person to pray for the item written on the index card.

ANSWERS TO BIBLE APPLICATION EXERCISES

1. God's Presence Revealed

a. God's presence was revealed in an angel calling out audibly to Abraham out of heaven.

b. An angel of the Lord wrestled with Jacob through the night and then blessed him.

c. God appeared as a flame of fire in a bush that burned but was not consumed.

d. The Lord came, stood, and called out audibly to Samuel.

e. The Lord spoke to Job out of a whirlwind.

f. SUMMARY ANSWER: We encounter God's presence in circumstances where we see the hand of God protecting and preserving where danger and peril could have done much more. The Columbine shootings could have been much worse. The 9/11 disaster could have been worse. These and other tragedies reveal that God has been at work. There may be other answers and examples.

2. God's Protection from Violence in the Old Testament

a. God protected Noah and his family because Noah found grace in the eyes of the Lord.

b. God sent angels to escort Lot from Sodom. They led Lot and his family out to safety and gave explicit instructions on how to escape the violence to come.

c. Saul's son, Jonathan, went to David and informed him of the danger to his life and encouraged David to hide so he would be safe. Jonathan also pleaded with his father on David's behalf.

d. God will provide a safe place from danger; He will deliver you from those who seek to catch and destroy you; and He will protect you from attackers and their weapons. Several other protections are also mentioned in this psalm.

e. God will keep watch over His people diligently and never sleep on the job; He will preserve His people from evil.

f. SUMMARY ANSWER: God protected the Columbine students from the bombs that the attackers had planted. He prevented more deaths by arranging circumstances that allowed the majority of students to escape the school.

3. God's Protection from Violence in the New Testament

a. God instructed Joseph in a dream to take the infant Jesus to Egypt to avoid the murder of the child by Herod.

b. In their anger over His teachings, the people in the synagogue in Jesus' hometown of Nazareth sought to throw Him over a cliff. God saved Jesus from this violence by bringing Him right through the midst of the crowd and sending Him on His way to His next destination, Capernaum.

c. Jesus confirmed in His prayer to God that He had protected all the disciples from harm except the "son of perdition," Judas.

d. The disciples saved Paul from those who sought to kill him by lowering him down a wall in a basket.

e. The church prayed "without ceasing" for Peter, and angels were then used by God to free him from prison.

f. SUMMARY ANSWER: The Christian should always keep in mind that "if our earthly house of this tabernacle were dissolved, we have a building of God, a house not made with hands, eternal in the heavens" (2 Corinthians 5:1).

4. God's Response to Violent Living

a. The earth was filled with violence, and God was determined to destroy it.

b. David was not allowed to build a temple to God because he had been a man of war and had shed blood.

c. God delivered David from his enemies and from violent men.

d. John the Baptist told the soldiers to "do violence to no man."

e. Jesus taught that those who use the sword will perish by the sword.

f. SUMMARY ANSWER: We should turn from violence and avoid the consequences of losing favor with God by promoting or engaging in violent behavior.

5. Violence and Life in the Spirit

a. This is a spiritual battle, and one that must be fought with spiritual weapons.

b. We need to guard our thoughts, bring them captive to the obedience of Christ, and be prepared to take positive steps to respond to media violence.

c. Young people should be encouraged to walk in the Spirit—to live a life that is led by the Spirit of God. Such a life produces the fruit of the spirit, not the violent works of the flesh.

d. The humility of Christ is the model for the Christian. We should have a mind–set that is spiritually prepared for whatever the world presents, and know that ultimately God will be glorified in the process.

e. A spirit of readiness to answer any who would question your faith prepares you for this.

f. SUMMARY ANSWER: The kingdom of heaven is forcefully (violently) advancing and forceful men lay hold to it (see Matthew 11:12). God expects the same zeal that is shown by the violent men or women to be used by the godly men and women to advance His Kingdom.

6. Ministry Application

The subject of gun control should be considered by the church. Though laws vary by state and city, and many areas have customs and traditions that include lawful use and possession of weapons, all communities have an interest in the avoidance of unlawful use and possession of weapons. Education and training about gun safety can save lives in a church and in a community.

CHAPTER SEVEN

TELEVISION— Hip-Hop and Sin

Format for Sessions of 90 Minutes or More

PART ONE		PART TWO*	
MIN.	ACTIVITY	MIN.	ACTIVITY
5	Prayer	5	Case Study
10	Personal Reflections	30	Small Group Study
15	Scripture Discussion	10	Small Group Presentations
10	Chapter Highlights	18	Large Group Discussion
		3	Prayer

For sessions of less than 90 minutes, use PART ONE only, and assign the case study as homework. *To complete the activities in PART TWO, each participant will need to use the workbook that accompanies the student book.

LESSON AIM: At the end of this two-part training session, the participant should be able to: a) understand God's view of sin; b) describe how television promotes sin; c) explain how hip-hop culture has been used to promote sin; d) discuss how the media misrepresents African American culture more negatively than reality; e) identify biblical passages that explain sin and God's response to it.

I. PART ONE

A. PRAYER

At the beginning of the session, have each student think of an area of sin, personal change, or difficulty they are currently struggling with. Open the session with prayer including the reminder that 1 John 1:9 promises that God will forgive us and that 1 Corinthians 10:13 promises that God will give us a way of escape from our temptations.

B. PERSONAL REFLECTIONS

Last time, participants were asked to make personal applications of the material covered in the last session, using exercise #7 of chapter six. Allow time for volunteers to share their reflections. Then introduce the lesson for today—Hip–Hop and Sin.

C. SCRIPTURE DISCUSSION

Read John 1:29; John 19:16–18; 1 Corinthians 15:3; and 1 John 1:7b. Then discuss the following questions:
1. What was the purpose of Jesus' coming according to John the Baptist?
2. Why was Jesus crucified?
3. What, if anything, did Jesus have in common with those who were killed with Him?
4. What was the purpose of Jesus' death according to 1 Corinthians 15:3?
5. What is the effect of the blood of Jesus?

D. CHAPTER HIGHLIGHTS

Explain that the chapter focuses on sin. Have the class participants give their definitions of sin. Explore the question of whether some sins are worse than others. Is listening to rap music sin? Is dancing a sin? Is it a sin to watch certain television programs? Using chapter seven as background, provide a general overview of the points made in the chapter. Be sure to include the following questions:
1. What is sin, and how does it affect our relationship with God?

2. What was the reason for the crucifixion of Christ?
3. What are some of the ways that television promotes sin?
4. How has African American music and dance culture been used to promote sin on television?
5. What should a Christian do to respond to sin on television?

Ask the group to reflect on Phil's situation (from the workbook case study). Ask them to share their experiences of witnessing to people who feel they are not sinners and how they may have approached this situation. Encourage participants to share how they personally came to realize that their righteousness was not good enough for God.

II. PART TWO

To complete the activities in PART TWO, each participant will need the workbook that accompanies the student book.

A. CASE STUDY

1. Introduction
The case study in the workbook provides an opportunity to apply the principles presented in the chapter to a real–life story. In the case study, Phil attempts to use the movie *The Passion of the Christ* as a tool to witness to his friend Sylvia. Sylvia believes she is a good person and does not need church to be spiritual.

2. Procedure
Select Small Group Leaders. Ask for volunteers or select five group leaders. Then assign each group leader a number (1–5). (This can be done beforehand.) Ask each group leader to write their number on a large sheet of paper so that it can easily be seen.

Divide into Small Groups. Inform the participants that they will assemble into five small groups. Each group will study a different set of questions relat-

ed to the case study and will present their findings to the larger group at the end of the group study period. The set of questions to be studied should correspond with the group numbers as follows:

Group #1: God's Word on Sin
Group #2: The Holiness of God
Group #3: Television Promotes Sin
Group #4: Sin and "Good" People
Group #5: From Sin to Transformation

Ask the class to count off by fives. Then ask them to join the small group leader that is displaying their respective assigned number. Inform them of the meeting places for each of the groups. (These locations can be printed beforehand to facilitate a smoother transition.) Then allow the participants to assemble into smaller groups at their designated meeting places.

B. SMALL GROUP STUDY

1. Small Group Leaders Allocate Questions

For each exercise, there are five "discovery" questions and a summary question. Assign each person one of the discovery questions. If there are more people than questions, allow people to work on questions in twos or threes, etc. If there are more questions than people, assign more than one question per person.

Don't consider the summary question at this time; the entire small group will discuss it at the end of the small group discussion time, and it will be used as a basis for the group presentation to the larger group. Ask each person (or pair, etc.) to answer the assigned question.

2. Share Insights

After 10 minutes, ask the small group participants to come together in their groups. Allow each one to tell the question that he/she had and his/her answer to it. Allow 5–18 minutes to discuss the summary question as a group. Then ask for a volunteer to summarize the small group discussion and report when the larger group reconvenes. Remind the designated person that he/she will only have one minute to present.

C. LARGE GROUP PRESENTATIONS

1. Large Group Leader

Reconvene the Group. Call the small groups back together. If they are in different locations of the building, consider sending a designated person to each location or selecting another method of notifying them that time is up.

Explain the Procedure. Explain that a representative of each small group will share that group's reflections on Phil and Sylvia and the movie *The Passion of the Christ* with the larger group. Then the large group, together, can discuss a final summary exercise and reflect together on making a practical application of what has been learned.

Remind Small Group Representatives of the Time. Remind each small group representative that they should try to summarize their group's discussion in one minute. Be sure that the small group presenters connect their group presentations both to the case study and the information in the chapter. The respective small group emphasis should be on helping to recognize that:

Group #1: God condemns sin and demands a sacrifice

Group #2: God is holy and beyond the reach of man's righteousness

Group #3: Television promotes sin and the Bible has prophesied more sinfulness

Group #4: There is no one who is "good enough" to reach God on their own

Group #5: The Bible shows us the path from sin to transformation

Be sure that they relate some of the Scriptures from the exercises to each of the topics above.

2. Ministry Application

The purpose of this exercise is to identify ways in which the television viewing habits of church members can influence their conduct and how a church can more effectively minister through understanding the media's

influence on its members. Use the worksheet in the workbook to guide the discussion and as a basis for summarizing it on newsprint, chalkboard, or an overhead transparency.

3. Personal Application

Ask participants, between this session and the next, to reflect on the Personal Application (exercise #7) and to read chapter eight. Call their attention to the section in their workbooks that can be used for journalizing. Also ask them to reflect on the questions at the end of chapter eight in their student books in preparation for the next session.

D. PRAYER

Hold hands and, in a circle, ask for specific prayer requests. Then ask for several volunteers to pray while keeping the prayer requests in mind.

ANSWERS TO BIBLE APPLICATION EXERCISES

1. God's Word on Sin

a. The penalty for sin in Genesis 2:16–17 was death.

b. God's anger could be kindled, and you could be destroyed from the face of the earth.

c. God promised that man would be cursed, confused, and rebuked in everything that his hand was put to until he was destroyed. More consequences are described in later verses in this passage, including physical illnesses.

d. Jesus came to fulfill the law not to abolish it and said that not the smallest letter of the law would disappear until heaven and earth disappear.

e. The Holy Spirit will convict the world of sin because of unbelief in Jesus Christ.

f. SUMMARY ANSWER: The purpose of the law was to bring us to Christ. The law could not justify man before God; Scripture has concluded that all have sinned, so we must be justified by faith in Christ not by keeping the law.

2. The Holiness of God

a. There is none like God, glorious in holiness, fearful in praises, doing wonders.

b. God speaks in His holiness.

c. The whole earth is full of God's glory; He is holy.

d. The Lord is righteous and holy in all His works.

e. The Lord was a holy Father to Christ and is to us as well.

f. SUMMARY ANSWER: We should approach God in absolute reverence, knowing that His holiness far exceeds our greatest righteousness and goodness (see also Isaiah 64:6).

3. Television Promotes Sin

a. Jesus said that we would hear about wars, famines, pestilences, and earthquakes from around the world.

b. Reports of homosexuality, hedonism, and false religious beliefs and practices are commonly found on television news and in current events.

c. The Christian is encouraged to put off the corrupt ways of the world and to walk in a new life created after God in holiness.

d. The Christian should expose the works of evil present in the world and have nothing to do with them.

e. The believer should live to please God and behave in a way that is holy and honorable.

f. SUMMARY ANSWER: Phil should carefully consider whether or not a movie or television program can effectively convey the message of the Gospel. The entertainment uses of media may make it difficult to establish a serious dialogue about the Christian faith. There may be an opportunity with the movie *The Passion of the Christ*, but he must carefully consider the person he is trying to reach and the message he hopes to communicate.

4. Sin and "Good" People

It is important for Sylvia to realize that all have sinned and come short of the glory of God. No sin is seen as superior to another sin in God's eyesight. No one in the church or out of the church can claim superiority over anyone.

We are not saved according to the works that we did or did not do. We are saved only by the grace of God.

a. All of us are like lost sheep and have turned to our own wicked ways.
b. Our righteousness must exceed that of the most religious men of Jesus' day or we will not enter the kingdom of heaven.
c. Jesus challenges us to not only love those who love us but to love our enemies also and to be "perfect" as God is perfect.
d. There is no one who is truly righteous and truly seeks after God.
e. All have sinned and fall short of God's glory.
f. SUMMARY ANSWER: No one will be justified by the works of the law.

5. From Sin to Transformation
a. Transform your thinking and present yourself to God.
b. Be careful how you live because the days are evil.
c. Think about things that are lovely, pure, true, and right.
d. Set your mind on heavenly things not earthly things.
e. Avoid every kind of evil.
f. SUMMARY ANSWER: Evil desires unchecked give birth to sin, which results in death. Phil should consider using the Word of God to establish the pattern of sin and redemption through the perfect work of Jesus Christ. The crucifixion was the beginning of the end result of Christ's fulfillment of the law and the resurrection and eternal life available to all who believe. Using the direction given in the Scriptures, Phil should show how a life of godliness is the result of accepting Christ's sacrifice, repentance, and salvation followed by the leading of the Holy Spirit and the discipline of a mind focused on pleasing God.

6. Ministry Application
Surveys, if done in an anonymous fashion, can be informative and provide direction for ministry programs. It is possible that the viewing habits of a church family can have a direct impact on the problems a congregation is facing. Television is influential and does change behavior. Look for indications that evil ideas or worldly beliefs may have crept into the church through the casual viewing of wicked programs.

CHAPTER EIGHT

TELEVISION–
Life After Death

Format for Sessions of 90 Minutes or More

PART ONE		PART TWO*	
MIN.	ACTIVITY	MIN.	ACTIVITY
5	Prayer	5	Case Study
10	Personal Reflections	25	Small Group Study
5	Scripture Discussion	10	Small Group Presentations
20	Chapter Highlights	15	Large Group Discussion
		5	Prayer

*For sessions of less than 90 minutes, use PART ONE only, and assign the case study as homework. *For PART TWO activities, participants will need the workbook that accompanies the student book.*

LESSON AIM: At the end of this two–part training session, the participant should be able to: a) describe the events of the Resurrection of Jesus Christ; b) understand the importance of belief in the Resurrection; c) discuss the proof of the Resurrection described in Scripture; and d) respond to the television depictions of life after death with the facts and truths of Scripture.

I. PART ONE

A. PRAYER

Open the session with prayer, including the lesson aim.

B. PERSONAL REFLECTIONS

Last time, participants were asked to make personal applications of the material covered in the last session, using exercise #7 of chapter seven. Allow time for volunteers to share the results of this Personal Application. Then introduce the lesson for today—Life After Death.

C. SCRIPTURE DISCUSSION

Read John 20:11–29 and Acts 1:3. Alternate between leader and group. Then discuss the following questions:

1. What questions did the angel ask Mary at the tomb?
2. How do we know that Mary did not perceive them as angels?
3. What was Mary's response upon seeing the resurrected Christ?
4. What were Jesus' instructions to Mary?
5. What proof did Jesus offer the disciples to confirm His identity?
6. What was the significance of the locked doors in the room where the disciples met?
7. Describe Jesus' encounter with Thomas. What were the key events in this meeting?

D. CHAPTER HIGHLIGHTS

Using chapter eight as background, provide a general overview of the points made in the chapter. Be sure to discuss the following questions:

1. What is the event that sets Christianity apart from other faiths?
2. What are television's typical approaches to life after death?
3. How can we be influenced by these television images?
4. When does a negative focus on the realm of the Spirit influence our faith?

Ask the group to relate what they may know about the afterlife beliefs of different faiths (from the workbook case study). Ask what they believe will

happen to them immediately after death. Be sure to ask for scriptural support for their beliefs.

II. PART TWO

To complete the PART TWO activities, each participant will need the workbook that accompanies the student book.

A. CASE STUDY

1. Introduction

Explain that the case study in the workbook provides an opportunity to apply the principles presented in the chapter to a real–life story. Mother Williams, in the case study, must discuss the Resurrection with her grandson. He is returning from college with questions about life after death that were raised in his Comparative Religions class. She needs to be able to provide scriptural support for what she has taught him over the years.

2. Procedure

Select Small Group Leaders. Ask for volunteers or select five group leaders. Then assign each group leader a number (1–5). (This can also be done beforehand.) Ask each group leader to write their number on a large sheet of paper so that it can be seen from a distance.

Divide into Small Groups. Inform the group of participants that they will be broken down into five small groups. Each group will study a different set of questions that can be related to the case study, and will present their findings to the larger group at the end of the small group study period. The set of questions in the workbook to be studied should correspond with the numbers of the groups as follows:

Group #1: Mary Encounters the Resurrected Christ
Group #2: The Disciples Encounter the Resurrected Christ
Group #3: Jesus Appears to Thomas
Group #4: The Resurrected Jesus Christ

Group #5: Christianity Requires Resurrection

Have the participants count off by fives. Then ask them to join the small group leader that is displaying their respective assigned number. Inform them of the meeting places for each of the five groups. (These locations can also be printed beforehand to facilitate a smoother meeting time.) Then allow the participants to assemble into the small groups at their designated meeting places.

B. SMALL GROUP STUDY

1. Small Group Leaders Allocate Questions

For each exercise, there are five "discovery" questions and a summary question. Therefore, each small group will have one exercise to complete and that exercise will involve answering five questions and a summary question. Assign one discovery question to each person in the group. If there are more people than questions, allow people to work on questions in twos or threes, etc. If there are more questions than people, assign more than one question per person.

Don't consider the summary question at this time; it will be discussed by the small group at the end of the group study time, and it will be used as a basis for the small group presentation to the larger group.

Ask each person (or pair, etc.) to answer the assigned question.

2. Share Insights

After 10 minutes, ask the small group participants to come together in their groups. Allow each one to tell the question that they had and their answer to it. Then allow 5–18 minutes to discuss the summary question as a group. Designate someone who will summarize the small group discussion and report to the larger group. Remind the designated person that he/she will only have one minute to present.

C. LARGE GROUP PRESENTATIONS

1. Large Group Leader

Reconvene the Group. Call the small groups back together. If they are in different locations of the building, consider sending a designated person around to each location or selecting another method of notifying them that time is up.

Explain the Procedure. Explain that a representative of each small group will share that group's reflections on the Resurrection with the larger group. Inform them that following the small group presentations, the larger group can reflect on a practical application of what has been learned by discussing the Ministry Application.

Remind Small Group Representatives of the Time. Remind each small group representative that they should try to summarize their group's discussion in one minute. Be sure that the small group presenters connect their small group presentations both to the case study of Mother Williams and the chapter. The respective small group emphasis should be on:

Group #1: The encounter Mary has with the Resurrected Christ
Group #2: The encounter the disciples have with the Resurrected Christ
Group #3: The encounter Thomas has with the Resurrected Christ
Group #4: Jesus' other appearances after His resurrection
Group #5: The Christian's response to the Resurrection

Be sure that they relate some of the Scriptures from the exercises to each of the topics above.

2. Ministry Application

Ask each participant to locate the Ministry Application worksheet in his/her workbook.

Have one or more of the groups present their play to the entire class. Discuss the meaning of the Resurrection as presented by the groups' plays.

3. Personal Application

Call the participants' attention to the spaces for journalizing in the workbook. Ask them during the upcoming week to meditate on the questions and related Scriptures, and write their private thoughts in the spaces provided in the workbook. Encourage them to read chapter nine in preparation for the next session and reflect on the discussion and Scripture study questions at the end of the chapter.

D. PRAYER

Hold hands and, in a circle, ask for specific prayer requests, particularly for abandoned people that they know. Then ask for several volunteers to pray, keeping the prayer requests in mind.

ANSWERS TO BIBLE APPLICATION EXERCISES

1. Mary Encounters the Resurrected Christ

a. Mary went to the tomb very early in the morning, just before daybreak.

b. She was going with spices to anoint Jesus' body.

c. Mary was accompanied by Mary, mother of James, and Salome, or Joanna.

d. Mary first reported that Jesus' body had been taken. Peter and John ran to see what had happened.

e. Jesus told Mary to tell the disciples that He, "was returning to my Father and your Father, to my God and your God."

f. SUMMARY ANSWER: The differences in the four accounts all add to the story and do not contradict each other. Each writer includes some details that the others do not, reflecting the harmony and the complementary nature of the Gospels.

2. The Disciples Encounter the Resurrected Christ

a. Peter and John (the disciple that "Jesus loved") were the first to come to the tomb.

b. The disciples went into the tomb, saw the grave clothes, and returned home.

c. Jesus appeared before the disciples through a closed and locked door in a room where they had gathered.

d. Jesus showed the disciples His pierced hands and side to prove His identity, and the disciples responded with joy.

e. Jesus' messages were: 1) Peace be with you; 2) As the Father has sent me, I am sending you; and 3) Receive the Holy Spirit.

f. SUMMARY ANSWER: Mother Williams can discuss these Scriptures with Brandon, emphasizing that these reliable accounts were written while the eyewitnesses to these events were still living. The Scriptures speak of the

truth of the Resurrection and the events of Jesus' last days on earth before His ascension.

3. Jesus Appears to Thomas

a. The disciples told Thomas that they had seen the Lord. Thomas did not believe them and said he would believe only if he could actually touch and examine Jesus' injuries from the crucifixion.

b. Thomas was with the disciples a week later when Jesus appeared.

c. Jesus spoke directly to Thomas and commanded him to put his fingers in Jesus' hands and side.

d. Thomas testified that Jesus was both his Lord and God.

e. Jesus responded that Thomas was blessed because he had seen and believed and blessed are those who have not seen and yet have believed.

f. SUMMARY ANSWER: These Scriptures were written that people would believe in Jesus Christ (John 20:30). They provide eyewitness accounts that can be used to validate the claims of Christ and those who believe in His Resurrection.

4. The Resurrected Jesus Christ

a. Jesus was on earth for 40 days after His Resurrection.

b. Jesus had a physical body that could be touched, and He ate meals in the presence of those who saw Him.

c. Jesus explained that His Resurrection was a fulfillment of what He told them before His crucifixion and was a fulfillment of the prophecies of the Old Testament.

d. In His third appearance to the disciples, Jesus encounters them on a fishing trip. There were seven of the disciples present including Peter, Thomas, Nathanael, the sons of Zebedee, and two others.

e. Over 500 people saw Jesus after His Resurrection.

f. SUMMARY ANSWER: Jesus appeared to His disciples and over 500 others after His Resurrection. He had a physical body that could be touched and held, and He also ate food with them. Jesus' body apparently had other properties, which allowed Him to appear and disappear at will and to transport Himself to other places. These eyewitness accounts, record-

ed in the Scriptures at a time when many were still living, conclusively prove His Resurrection.

5. Christianity Requires Resurrection

a. Paul recounts the actual appearances of Jesus after His Resurrection and points out that many of the witnesses are still living at the time of his writing. Significantly, Paul counts his encounter with Jesus on the Damascus Road as a postresurrection appearance of Christ.

b. Without the Resurrection, the Christian faith is useless. If Christ was not resurrected, then neither would we be resurrected.

c. By Adam, death came into the world, but through Christ all can be made alive.

d. Using the analogy of seed, Paul pointed out that to each kind of seed God gives a unique body.

e. The resurrected body will be imperishable, glorious, powerful, and spiritual. Jesus demonstrated these characteristics in each of His appearances, in which He came suddenly into locked rooms, traveled across distances, and ultimately ascended into heaven.

f. SUMMARY ANSWER: Reincarnation would mean that Jesus' sacrifice for sin was meaningless since it could not stop the endless cycle of rebirth that reincarnation teaches. The teaching of 1 Corinthians 15 makes it clear that humans can only produce humans, not animals or other forms.

6. Ministry Application

The use of drama can be a very effective teaching approach, even with adults. Having students act out stories of the Resurrection can be a powerful tool to teach the truths of these lessons. A more detailed project would be the analysis of other religions and examination of the distinctions between what Christians believe and the views of others.

CHAPTER NINE

TELEVISION—God's People at Worship

Format for Sessions of 90 Minutes or More

PART ONE		PART TWO	
MIN.	ACTIVITY	MIN. *	ACTIVITY
5	Prayer	5	Case Study
10	Personal Reflections	30	Small Group Study
15	Scripture Discussion	10	Small Group Presentations
10	Chapter Highlights	18	Large Group Discussion
		3	Prayer

For sessions of less than 90 minutes, use PART ONE only, and assign the case study as homework. *To complete the activities in PART TWO, each participant will need the workbook that accompanies the student book.

LESSON AIM: At the end of this two–part training session, the participant should be able to: a) define worship and distinguish worship from praise; b) understand what true worship requires; c) discuss the need for and requirement of fellowship among believers; d) discuss the connection between worship and giving; e) discuss the issues surrounding worship and television ministries.

I. PART ONE

A. PRAYER

Open the session with prayer, including the lesson aim.

B. PERSONAL REFLECTIONS

Last time, participants were asked to make personal applications of the material covered in the last session, using exercise #7 of chapter eight. Allow time for volunteers to share the results of this Personal Application. Then introduce the lesson for today—God's People at Worship.

C. SCRIPTURE DISCUSSION

Read Psalms 95:1–7; 100; 119:11; Philippians 4:6; Romans 10:14; and 1 Corinthians 16:1–2. Alternate between leader and group. Then discuss the following questions:
1. Why should we worship God?
2. What aspects of creation cause us to want to worship God?
3. What are some actions of worship described in the Psalms?
4. How can we avoid sinning against God?
5. What is the cure for cares and anxiety?

D. CHAPTER HIGHLIGHTS

Explain that the chapter focuses on worship—its meaning, purpose, and practice. Bring to class a large poster board, newsprint, or use the chalkboard. Ask each person to go to the board to write a practice or behavior that he/she would associate with worship. Discuss the different practices or behaviors and what each person thinks makes them pleasing to God. Review the definition of worship given in the chapter and the distinction between praise and worship. Give an overview of the points made in the chapter. Be sure to discuss the following questions:
1. What did Jesus mean by worshiping in "spirit and in truth"?
2. Do location and numbers of people make a difference in worship?
3. Why does God want believers to come together?
4. What is the connection between worship and giving?

5. What is wrong with only worshiping in front of a televised service?

Ask the group to consider Sandra's situation (from the workbook case study) and give examples of what they would consider appropriate or inappropriate worship. Be sure to explore the reasons for their views and apply the Scriptures discussed in the chapter to the responses.

II. PART TWO

To complete the activities in PART TWO, each participant will need the workbook that accompanies the student book.

A. CASE STUDY
1. Introduction
Explain that the case study is an opportunity to apply the principles presented in the chapter to a real–life story. Sandra, in the case study, is concerned about worship at her brother's church.

2. Procedure
Select Small Group Leaders. Ask for volunteers or select five group leaders. Then assign each group leader a number (1–5). (This can also be done beforehand.) Ask each group leader to write their number on a large sheet of paper so that it can be seen from a distance.

Divide into Small Groups. Inform the participants that they will be forming five small groups. Each group will study a different set of questions related to the case study and will present their findings to the larger group at the end of the group study period. The set of questions to be studied should correspond with the group numbers as follows:
Group #1: Jesus' Teachings on Worship
Group #2: Corporate and Private Worship
Group #3: Worship and Praise
Group #4: Sacrifice and Worship
Group #5: Worship and Dance

Have the participants count off by fives. Then ask them to join the small group leader that is displaying their assigned number. Inform them of the meeting places for each of the groups. (These locations can also be printed beforehand to facilitate a smoother transition.) Then allow the participants to assemble into the smaller groups at their designated meeting places.

B. SMALL GROUP STUDY
1. Small Group Leaders Allocate Questions

For each exercise, there are five "discovery" questions and a summary question. Therefore, each small group has one exercise to complete and that exercise will involve answering five questions and the summary question. Assign one discovery question to each person in the group. If there are more people than questions, allow people to work on questions in twos or threes, etc. If there are more questions than people, assign more than one question per person. Don't consider the summary question at this time; the small group will discuss it at the end of the group study time, and it will be used as a basis for the small group presentation to the larger group. Ask each person (or pair, etc.) to answer the assigned question.

2. Share Insights

After 10 minutes, ask the small group participants to come together in their groups. Allow each one to tell the question that he/she had and his/her answer to it. Then allow 5–18 minutes to discuss the summary question as a group. Designate someone who will summarize the small group discussion and report to the larger group. Remind the designated person that he/she will only have one minute to present.

C. LARGE GROUP PRESENTATIONS
1. Large Group Leader

Reconvene the Group. Call the small groups back together. If the groups are in different locations of the building, consider sending a designated person around to each location or selecting another method of notifying them that time is up.

Explain the Procedure. Explain that a representative of each small group

will share that group's reflections on Sandra's situation with the larger group. Then the large group can discuss the Ministry Application and reflect together on making a practical application of what has been learned.

Remind Small Group Representatives of the Time. Remind each small group representative that he/she should try to summarize their group's discussion in one minute. Be sure that the small group presenters connect group presentations both to the case study of Sandra and to others who may be trying to decide what is and is not appropriate worship. Many churches are changing their practices of worship while many people are spending more and more time watching television ministries. The respective small group emphasis should be on:

Group #1: What Jesus taught about worship
Group #2: Examples of corporate and private worship in Scripture
Group #3: Examples of worship and praise in Scripture
Group #4: Examples of sacrifice and worship in Scripture
Group #5: Worship and dance in Scripture

Be sure that they relate some of the Scriptures from the exercises to each of the topics above.

2. Ministry Application

Consider reviewing the worship and praise ministries of your church as a group using the Scriptures covered as a point of reference. Many churches are exploring new ways of worship. What does the biblical example say?

3. Personal Application

Ask them, between this session and the next, to reflect on the Personal Application in the workbook. Call their attention to the spaces for journalizing to be used for this purpose.

D. PRAYER

Hold hands and, in a circle, ask for specific prayer requests. Then ask for several volunteers to pray while keeping the prayer requests in mind.

ANSWERS TO BIBLE APPLICATION EXERCISES

1. Jesus' Teachings on Worship

a. True worshipers only worship God.

b. Jesus taught that only God should be worshiped and not the things put in front of us by the world and the devil.

c. Jesus asked God to glorify Him (or give honor/worship) just as God had done when they were together in heaven. Jesus is God and both are worthy of worship.

d. God seeks worshipers who are sincerely worshiping Him in spirit and in truth.

e. Jesus taught that the place of worship was less important than the heart of the worshiper.

f. SUMMARY ANSWER: Leon appears to be the truest worshiper since we have evidence that he has moved to serve God through his efforts in the prison ministry. Sandra could be a worshiper; we do not have enough facts to really know. It seems that she may be avoiding communal worship.

2. Corporate and Private Worship

a. The people bowed down, worshiped, and praised the Lord, and then offered sacrifices to God.

b. The people gathered together, read the Scriptures, lifted their hands, and bowed their heads in worship to God.

c. Job shaved his head, tore his clothes, and worshiped God. Worship is the best response to adversity.

d. David illustrates the appropriateness of worship in times of trial when he worships after learning of the death of his child from Bathsheba. He prepared for worship by washing, putting on clean clothes, and anointing himself.

e. Music, singing, and prayers are offered in worship at the throne of God.

f. SUMMARY ANSWER: Her brother's church seems closer to the model of worship in the Scriptures. (There is no right or wrong answer here.)

3. Worship and Praise

a. Hannah praises God for answering her prayer and giving her a son, Samuel, after a period of barrenness.

b. Deborah and Barak praise God after a victory over the King of Canaan.

c. Daniel praises God for giving him the secret dream that Nebuchadnezzar dreamed and the meaning of the dream.

d. The people praise God for Jesus upon His entrance into Jerusalem.

e. The early church celebrates in praise to God.

f. SUMMARY ANSWER: It is likely that the praise and worship in these examples lasted much longer.

4. Sacrifice and Worship

a. Abraham said that he was going to worship as he went to fulfill God's command to sacrifice his son.

b. God gives instructions on sacrifice and worship.

c. Peninnah and Hannah went to the temple yearly to sacrifice and worship.

d. Elijah's sacrifice is received on Mount Carmel and the people worship God.

e. Hezekiah leads the people in sacrifices and praise to God.

f. SUMMARY ANSWER: We are encouraged to present our bodies as a living sacrifice.

5. Worship and Dance

a. Miriam and all the women danced.

b. The women danced, sang, and played tambourines.

c. David danced before the Lord with all his might.

d. The psalmist says to praise the name of God in dance.

e. Praise God with tambourines and dancing.

f. SUMMARY ANSWER: Leon can give some scriptural support for praise dancers in his church. His sister's concerns about the dancers' attire are not addressed in these texts.

6. Ministry Application

Answers will vary as you review your church's worship practices.

CHAPTER TEN

TELEVISION—The World of Reality

Format for Sessions of 90 Minutes or More

PART ONE		PART TWO	
MIN.	ACTIVITY	MIN.	ACTIVITY
5	Prayer	5	Case Study
10	Personal Reflections	30	Small Group Study
15	Scripture Discussion	10	Small Group Presentations
10	Chapter Highlights	18	Large Group Discussion
		3	Prayer

*For sessions of less than 90 minutes, use PART ONE only, and assign the case study as homework. *To complete the activities in PART TWO, each participant will need the workbook that accompanies the student book.*

LESSON AIM: At the end of this two–part training session, the participant should be able to: a) describe the ministry of Barnabas; b) understand how television and media can distort our images of people and our ability to see the best in others; c) understand the need to make a commitment to live the Gospel in our daily lives; d) commit to loving God, loving our neighbors, and leading others to the truth of the Gospel.

I. PART ONE

A. PRAYER

If possible, music should precede the prayer. This can be done by bringing a CD player or an audiocassette player and playing music with which the group can sing along. Or, if a piano is available, ask for a volunteer to play a song that can lead into prayer. Then open the session with prayer, including the lesson aim in the prayer.

B. PERSONAL REFLECTIONS

Last time, participants were asked to make personal applications of the material covered in the last session, using exercise #7 of chapter nine. Allow time for volunteers to share the results of this Personal Application. Then introduce the lesson for today—The World of Reality.

C. SCRIPTURE DISCUSSION

Read Acts 4:36–37; 11:24–30. Alternate between leader and group. Then discuss the following questions:

1. How did Barnabas demonstrate his commitment to the work of the apostles?
2. Why was Joseph called Barnabas, and what was the meaning of the name?
3. How was Barnabas described in Acts 11:24?
4. What were the results of Barnabas' work in the ministry?
5. What are some indications of the disciples' trust of Barnabas?

D. CHAPTER HIGHLIGHTS

Explain that the chapter focuses on practical aspects of living the Christian life. Ask the class to provide examples of people who are visibly living the Christian life through their love of God and service to others. Be sure to solicit examples from within your ministry or fellowship as well as public figures nationally or in your community. Call to their attention the issues in the student book concerning television that could change how people feel about what is important in life and what God wants us to do with people. Then, using chapter ten as background, provide a general overview of the points made in the chapter. Be sure to include the following topics:

1. How can we see people through God's eyes, always looking for the best?
3. What are some ways that television can influence our thoughts about people?
4. What does the Scripture teach about managing our thought life? How might this apply to television viewing?
5. What does it mean to love and lead from the perspective of Jesus' words in Matthew 22:37–39 and 28:19–20?

Ask them to reflect on Tom Skinner's life (from the workbook case study). What are some of the things that he did that illustrate his Christian lifestyle? What can each student do to follow this example? Explore how the points presented in the chapter might apply to the participants' lives.

II. PART TWO

To complete the PART TWO activities, each participant will need the workbook that accompanies the student book.

A. CASE STUDY

1. Introduction

Explain that the case study in the workbook provides an opportunity to apply the principles presented in the chapter. In this case, Tom Skinner was a true example of a modern–day Barnabas. Though his life ended from cancer in his early fifties, his impact on individuals and ministries continues to this day.

2. Procedure

Select Small Group Leaders. Ask for volunteers or select five group leaders. Then assign each group leader a number (1–5). (This can also be done beforehand.) Ask each leader to write their number on a large sheet of paper so that it can be seen from a distance.

Divide into Small Groups. Inform the participants that they will be forming five small groups. Each group will study a different set of questions related to the case study, and will present their findings to the larger group at the end of the group study period. The set of questions to be studied should correspond with the numbers as follows:

Group #1: Putting Your Money Where Your Faith Is
Group #2: Bringing Thoughts into Obedience
Group #3: Loving God
Group #4: Loving Your Neighbor
Group #5: Leading Them to Christ

Have the participants count off by fives. Then ask them to join the small group leader that is displaying their assigned number. Inform them of the meeting places for each of the five groups. (These locations can be printed beforehand, to facilitate a smoother transition.) Allow the participants to assemble into groups at their designated meeting places.

B. SMALL GROUP STUDY

1. Small Group Leaders Allocate Questions

Each small group will complete one of the five exercises in the workbook. For each exercise, there are five "discovery" questions and a summary question. Therefore, the small group can divide into smaller groups, with one or more people assigned to each question from their assigned exercise.

If there are more people than questions, allow people to work on questions in twos or threes, etc. If there are more questions than people, assign more than one question per person. Don't consider the summary question at this time. The small group will discuss it at the end of the group study time, and it will be used as a basis for the small group presentation to the larger group. Ask each person (or pair, etc.) to answer the assigned question.

2. Share Insights

After 10 minutes, ask the small group participants to come together in their groups. Allow each to state the question that he/she had and his/her answer to it. Then allow 5–18 minutes to discuss the summary question as a group. Designate someone who will summarize the entire small group discussion when the larger group reconvenes. Remind the designated person that he/she will have only one minute to present.

C. LARGE GROUP PRESENTATIONS

1. Large Group Leader

Reconvene the Group. Call the small groups back together. If they are in different locations, consider sending someone to each location or selecting another method of notifying them that time is up.

Explain the Procedure. Explain that a representative of each small group will share that group's reflections on Tom Skinner's life with the larger group. Then the large group, together, can discuss the Ministry Application.

Remind Small Group Representatives of the Time. Remind each small group representative that he/she should try to summarize his/her group's discussion in one minute. Be sure that the small group presenters connect their presentations both to the case study of Tom Skinner and people who are similar to him. At this point, it shouldn't be necessary to spend much time with this because the group should be very familiar with the format by now. The respective small group emphasis should be:

Group #1: Showing your faith through your financial focus
Group #2: Guarding your thought life
Group #3: Demonstrating your love of God
Group #4: Showing love to your neighbor
Group #5: Becoming an effective evangelist

Be sure that they relate some of the Scriptures from the exercises to each of the topics above.

2. Ministry Application

Call attention to the worksheets in the workbook. After allowing about 5–7 minutes to complete the worksheets, ask for volunteers to present their answers.

3. Personal Application

Ask people to comment on what they have gained from this closer look at television from the perspective of Scripture. What have they changed as a result of this study? How will they be more effective as Christians?

D. PRAYER

Have the class form a circle. Ask each person to state a prayer request, and ask the person standing to their right to be responsible for stating a one–sentence prayer that mentions the prayer request of the person on their left.

ANSWERS TO BIBLE APPLICATION EXERCISES

1. Putting Your Money Where Your Faith Is

a. Jesus made it clear that we should store our treasures in heaven and reminded us that where our treasure is, our heart is also.

b. The rich ruler could not accept this teaching of Jesus and left this encounter sad because he had great wealth and did not want to let it go.

c. Jesus promised that those who left all for Him and the Gospel would receive a hundred times as much.

d. Jesus said that if you give, it will be given to you with the same measure that you gave.

e. Jesus said that you cannot serve both God and money.

f. SUMMARY ANSWER: Tom was clearly led to forsake the opportunities that his education and skills provided in order to make a difference for God's kingdom. Anyone who makes such choices must decide that pursuing power, wealth, or fame as a primary objective is at odds with God's commandment to choose a life that contributes to the kingdom.

2. Bringing Thoughts into Obedience

a. Television provides a constant flow of negative communication. The Scripture says that evil communications corrupt good manners.

b. The Bible says that as a person thinks within himself, so is he (KJV).

c. The battle for our minds is a spiritual war being waged by the devil.

d. We are encouraged to bring thoughts into captivity by demolishing thoughts and arguments that set themselves up against the knowledge of God.

e. We should think on those things that are pure, honest, and virtuous.

f. SUMMARY ANSWER: He could have been sidetracked by the Black Power movement, the sexual revolution, and the drug culture among other things.

3. Loving God

a. God's love will come from that person because out of the overflow of the heart, the mouth speaks.

b. People who love God keep His commandments.

c. People who do not love God do not keep His commandments.

d. Love the Lord your God with all your heart, soul, and mind.

e. God will love them and come and make His home with them.

f. SUMMARY ANSWER: Tom showed obedience to God in responding to His call to ministry and carrying out the work of the kingdom, reaching and teaching people.

4. Loving Your Neighbor

a. God commands that we should love our neighbors as ourselves in addition to loving Him.

b. Your neighbor is anyone in need who God places in your path, regardless of their race or ethnicity (see the story of the Good Samaritan).

c. Your neighbor can be your enemy since God gives us no credit for loving those we are obligated to love.

d. God promises a great reward for those who love this way.

e. God promises eternal punishment to those who refuse to demonstrate and accept His love.

f. SUMMARY ANSWER: His inner–city ministries, mentoring, and crusades are some of the ways he showed love for his neighbors.

5. Leading People to Christ

a. Jesus commanded that we should go and make disciples.

b. We should teach people to obey the things Jesus taught.

c. We should lead people who are close to us, nearby, and faraway. (Jerusalem, Judea, and Samaria and the uttermost parts of the world represent these areas faraway.)

d. No, Christ expects all believers to use their gifts to lead people into the kingdom (see, for example, John 4 and 1 Corinthians 12).

e. Praying is not enough; faith comes by hearing the Word of God. Someone has to speak the Word to the lost.

f. SUMMARY ANSWER: Television can be an important tool for evangelism, presenting the Gospel through preaching, teaching, and parables with powerful images.

6. Ministry Application

Discuss ways to implement the ministry plan for your neighborhood.

History of UMI (Urban Ministries, Inc.)

Urban Ministries, Inc.
The African American Christian Publishing & Communications Co.

The establishment of UMI (Urban Ministries, Inc.) was the fulfillment of a boyhood dream that Melvin E. Banks had at the age of 12. Soon after accepting Jesus Christ as his Savior, young Melvin gave his testimony on one of the back roads of Birmingham, Alabama. An old, white–haired Black man heard Melvin's testimony and quoted this verse to him: "My people are destroyed for lack of knowledge" (Hosea 4:6, KJV). This verse made a great impression on Melvin, and he was determined to yield himself to God so that he could be used to help bring the knowledge of His Word to Black people.

While working at Scripture Press, Melvin realized the need for resources that would appeal to urban Black Christians. In 1970, the Board of Directors was selected and Melvin's boyhood dream began to take shape with the incorporation of UMI.

During its first 12 years, UMI operated out of the basement of the Banks home. In 1982, UMI occupied the second floor of 1439 West 103rd Street in Chicago, Illinois. In 1985, UMI expanded its operation to include the first floor. In 1990, UMI moved to 1350 West 103rd Street in Chicago. In the spring of 1996, UMI completed construction and took occupancy of a new 21,000 square foot headquarters in the Chicagoland area.

The company's management philosophy encourages the development of employees for increased responsibilities and participation in most areas of the company's operations. In such a participative management style, building trust, loyalty, and confidence is essential for both management and employees.

The vision of a company where committed Christians can devote themselves to the preparation of Christ–centered resources continues to grow as UMI ministers to African Americans. The company is challenged to reach every Black Christian church with Christian education products and services. In accomplishing this mission, UMI recognizes its responsibility to our Lord, employees, customers, the community, and society.

Contact the Author

Contact author
C. Jeffrey Wright
UMI
(708) 868–7100
cjwright@urbanministries.com